RECALIBRATE!

Navigating the Job Market with Confidence

by Yvette Gavin

Recalibrate!
Navigating the Job Market with Confidence
Copyright © 2016 Yvette Gavin

First published by Faith Books & MORE

ISBN 978-1-939761-45-3

Printed in the United States of America

This book is printed on acid-free paper.

Faith Books & MORE
3255 Lawrenceville-Suwanee Rd.
Suite P250
Suwanee, GA 30024
publishing@faithbooksandmore.com
faithbooksandmore.com

Ordering Information:
Quantity sales. Special discounts are available on quantity purchases by corporations, associations, and others. For details, contact the publisher at the address above.

Orders by U.S. trade bookstores and wholesalers. Please contact Ingram Book Company: Tel: (800) 937-8000; Email: orders@ingrambook.com or visit ipage.ingrambook.com.

I dedicate this book to James.

From the time we met at Headline News (HLN) and married three years later, you have believed in me, supported my dreams, and been my biggest fan. This book is complete, in part, because you urged me to write it!

Acknowledgements

My special thanks go to **Candice Davis** who made my words sing on paper with her literary skills, **Nicole Smith** who published this book and brought everything together, and **Don Bolt** for the creative cover and layout design of this book.

Continual thanks go to **Pastor** and **Chaplain Andy Shepherd** who prays with me on Fridays, to **Jamison Gavin** who still to this day remains my WHY, and to **James, Mom, LaWanda, Wylene, Roberta, Denise, Courtney, Lucia, Bonnie,** and **Keith** who have consistently supported my dreams.

Table of Contents

What others are saying about YVETTE GAVIN

"…Yvette is all the mentor you need … great woman, highly competent, with an infectious spirit."

— **Jim Geiger,** former CEO and founder of Cbeyond

"I was fortunate to work with Yvette for several years during her Cbeyond career. She took over a QA organization that was working very hard, but struggling to deliver high quality solutions into production. Yvette drove significant organizational change in leveraging an offshore partnership and making strategic hires, she implemented significant process and automation changes that led to the group delivering increasingly higher quality at the same time the size of releases reached increased size and complexity. She was extremely committed to her team, the broader IT team, and Cbeyond as a whole, and I'm very proud to call her a friend!"

— **Joe Oesterling,** Executive Vice President at Liquid Web

"When Yvette came to Cbeyond, she instantly set about transforming our QA group and practices. She was very successful and the releases that her team verified had the highest levels of quality. On a professional basis, I would recommend her anywhere. She is, perhaps even more remarkable on a personal basis. Yvette "walks the walk" in terms of putting her beliefs and faith into practice on a daily basis."

— **Andrew Badstubner,** Chief Technology Officer at Kabbage, Inc.

"Yvette has been the most dynamic and charismatic leader I have worked for to date. She is extremely innovative, always brimming with new ideas to perform better. She is very inspirational to her team members and always pushes them to go that extra mile, earn that extra point which no one thought or believed they had the potential to achieve."

— **Srinath Narayanan,** Senior Manager

"I had the pleasure of working beside Yvette for several years, and can attest that she is one of the hardest and conscientious workers I have met. She excels at building a strong team and motivating her employees to meet their aggressive goals. Her people skills are top notch, and she is known as a great person to work for and with. Yvette brought in new structure and best practices to the Quality Assurance environment at Cbeyond, which was a direct contributor to increased productivity with the IT department."

— **Rick Klemm,** Director of Business Systems at Dell SecureWorks

"I had the pleasure of working with Yvette for several years during my tenure as Telecom Manager at Cbeyond Inc. Yvette worked with me as a Quality Control Director but was clearly much more than that. We worked on numerous projects, both big and small. But it was in our biggest project –the implementation of a new contact center IVR Solution – that Yvette and her team truly shined. During the implementation Yvette and her team worked closely with my team to qualify our changes were sound. Her methodical approach to ensure timely delivery of quality product to our customers is unmatched in my experience. Without her involvement, the project would have never achieved its goals. Finally, as a member of the IT team, Yvette was able to provide valuable input and recommendations for the direction of many of my projects. I found her to be an excellent sounding board and with her help, we were truly able to make changes in a direction that helped the company and the team."

— **Daniel E. Rodriguez,** Lead Driver - OCP Business Interiors Etc.

Introduction

Recalibrate | verb | *to check and adjust by comparison to a standard; to determine and make corrections in.*

"Don't look over," yelled Grasshopper, the pilot of the Napa Valley hot air balloon carrying my family and me. The descent from our exhilarating 4,100-foot flight had been going well when out of nowhere a sudden shift in wind direction moved the balloon directly over a tree planted in the middle of a vineyard—not a good place to land. In what seemed to be simultaneous maneuvers, Grasshopper radioed the ground crew for additional support and released more gas into the balloon envelope. This second action allowed him to recalibrate our landing position just enough to move the balloon slightly south of the tree. The landing was a little rough, but oh, what an adventure!

As it is with landing hot air balloons, landing a high-paying, fulfilling job you'll enjoy requires well-honed navigational skills. Just like that balloon ride, your career may not always go smoothly, but it should be an adventure you can look back on as a largely positive experience. It should be a journey you take charge of and control, just as our pilot controlled our flight. While you can't predict every change in direction, you can prepare yourself to pivot and perform so that, in the end, you arrive at a place where you have the privilege of going to your dream job every day. The right tools and the right support can help you maximize your chances of making that happen.

Recalibrate is your personal Global Positioning System (GPS), designed to help you navigate the hiring process with confidence, land the job you desire, earn the income you deserve, and continue to grow as a professional, all while enjoying the ride. Whether as a device in the car or an app on a mobile phone, you're likely familiar with GPS. This innovative tool helps millions of people get from where they are to where they want to go. Type in your location, and the computerized voice will tell you where to turn, predict how long it will take to reach your final destination, and announce the exact second of your arrival. Simple, right?

Well, in most cases, it is simple, but every so often you may get distracted and misunderstand the computerized voice. The appearance of familiar landmarks may lead you to veer off to take a route you think should be the right one. When this happens, the GPS quickly reassesses and adjusts the directions in an effort to get you back on track. This is when you hear the resounding, "Recalibrating! Recalibrating! Recalibrating!"

Throughout the years of navigating my own career path and coaching others to do the same, I've learned that most people have some sense of where they want to be. They drift along thinking they're on the right path until they look up and realize that years have passed and they're still pretty much in the same position with the same old income. Or worse, all those years have gone by, and with little or no warning, they're suddenly unemployed due to budget cuts or a company closing its doors. It happens far too often. Women are particularly vulnerable to this scenario because we tend to have so many obligations in other parts of our lives that we can easily lose sight of our career progress—or the lack thereof.

Whether you're looking to move up the corporate ladder, starting a new job search due to a layoff, or entering the workforce for the first time, Recalibrate will lay a course for you through the recruiting and hiring landscape, making it much easier for you to secure your dream job.

A Pair of Buster Browns

While the right skillset is critical to landing a great job, I've learned over time that it's not enough to set you apart from other candidates. Like most Americans, I was raised to believe if you were good at what you did you would be well rewarded for your dedication and excellent performance on the job. Experience has taught me that this isn't necessarily true. I have discovered that being the most skilled prospect for a position doesn't always yield the two words you want to hear: "You're hired!" Or "You're promoted!"

Years ago, early in my corporate career, I learned a tough lesson about the consequences of working hard without demanding fair compensation. Our budget was tight, but my husband and I went shopping for a new Easter outfit for our infant son. Growing up in my parents' home, Easter was one of the three occasions each year for which my siblings and I got new clothes (the others being Christmas and the first day of school), so this was a special moment for me. I was passing on a family tradition to my young son. And let's face it, Easter service is one for which many families like to show off their finest attire. We were no different.

We purchased an adorable little outfit, and I walked into a Buster Brown shoe store to find matching shoes. I gravitated toward the perfect pair, and I showed them to my husband. He looked at the shoes, and then he looked at me and said, "Yvette, we can't afford those shoes." That pair of baby shoes cost $32.

My husband and I both worked hard at our jobs. I went in every day, kept my nose to the grindstone, and produced more than many of my peers. In fact, I'd ended my maternity leave early to return to work when my boss offered me an opportunity to take on new accounts that I really wanted. Even after all that, I was standing in a shoe store unable to buy a relatively inexpensive pair of shoes I wanted for my baby.

We weren't living a lavish lifestyle, and I was accustomed to denying myself certain extras. But this was different. I wanted to give my son every single thing he needed, some of what he wanted, and much of what I wanted for him. I was working as hard as I could, but I wasn't seeing enough reward to make a material difference for my family. It was then I realized I had to make a change. I'll share more about how that situation turned out later, but suffice it to say that change didn't happen overnight. It took me a while to figure out exactly what to do, and I've continued to learn and implement more strategies over the years.

Fishing Lessons

For many years my family and friends have held me up as the example of someone with a talent for landing great jobs. After progressively more successful stints at several major companies including Delta Air Lines, Lockheed, Georgia Pacific, Coca-Cola Enterprises, AT&T, and Cox Communications, I began to consider that perhaps it wasn't all happenstance. Just maybe my family could be right about my ability. While my focus had always been securing the best job opportunities so I could help provide the lifestyle we wanted for our family, there was something more there. I'd developed a gift for steering my career in the direction I wanted it to go.

It wasn't until 2011, when a good friend called and asked me to coach her, that I fully realized how the techniques I applied during my own job searches and the things I'd learned as an interviewer and hiring manager could add real value to other people's career development. I took on the challenge and coached my friend for six weeks. We started by upgrading her professional appearance. Then we looked at what made her unique in the job market. She didn't know what that might be, but I pointed out the fact that she speaks five languages fluently. That's not a skillset you find every day. Even though a particular job might not require candidates to be multilingual, it's a real plus for many companies.

I helped her rewrite her resume to show that she had the necessary skills for the jobs for which she applied, but also to highlight her unique abilities in a way that made her stand out among other qualified candidates. After our coaching sessions, she landed a job with a major telecommunications company that paid her $50,000 more per year than her previous job. That's not a typo. She increased her annual salary by a full $50,000. Most of us would consider that a significant bump. While many employers are handing out 3% raises that get eaten up by taxes, it's possible to do a lot better.

This woman was a wife and mother, and the increase in salary happened just after a time when, like thousands of other Americans, her family had lost their home to foreclosure. Financially, it was a dark time for their household. However, she didn't sit back and hope someone would come along and throw more money at her. She reached out for help, and it meant so much to me to be the person who was able to assist her in making a difference for her career and, ultimately, for her family.

It would be great to be able to dole out cash whenever a friend needs it, but I realized I'd given her something more valuable. I'd helped her uncover the things she already had inside her that an employer would appreciate. I'd helped her develop the confidence she needed to walk into an interview and convince the hiring manager to choose her. I'd helped her take control of her career and her income. It was a clear example of the old saying, "If you give a man a fish, you feed him for a day, but teach a man to fish, and you feed him for life."

That was the beginning of my career-coaching practice. Since then, I've successfully coached clients into higher-paying jobs and more rewarding positions by showing them how to revamp their resumes, how to search for and identify jobs that aren't easily found, how to connect with decision-makers, and how to boldly share their experience and value during an interview.

In 2013, another client, who I'll call Barbara, successfully landed the information technology job of her dreams. For ten years she'd worked for the same company and grossed around $70,000 a year. After three months of working with me to identify opportunities and adjust specific aspects of her professional persona, Barbara increased her annual salary of $70,000 to $172,000. You're not misreading those numbers. Barbara more than doubled her income after a few months of recalibrating her approach to her job search. The increased pay was a huge win for her. But even bigger than the extra money was the increase in her confidence as I coached her through identifying and understanding her unique value. With that newly developed confidence, she can continue to grow her career and her income.

I have many more success stories, some of which I'll share with you throughout this book. My clients range from individuals with no experience and no college degree to those with many years of work experience and multiple advanced degrees. I've worked with people who were unemployed and underemployed, and the results have been the same. Each client has increased his or her salary and landed a job with the potential for more professional fulfillment and personal satisfaction.

In fact, for years now, my clients and family have urged me to write a book that outlines the strategies and techniques I've taught them so they could land the kinds of jobs that once seemed out of reach. They marvel at my knack for climbing the corporate ladder with grace. While I've watched people with two or three degrees and a much deeper pedigree than mine struggle to craft the careers they want, I've always managed to land fulfilling positions with great salaries in prestigious companies.

Based on my background, no one would've predicted I'd enjoy this level of professional success. I wasn't born with a silver spoon in my mouth, and I do not have an Ivy League education. I grew up in a working class family in the tiny town of Greenville, Georgia. How small was it? I attended the local public schools, and there were sixty students in my graduating class. After high school, I was fortunate enough to go away to college, but because of a family crisis that required me to return home in my senior year, I never completed that undergraduate degree. It was a credential I couldn't claim when I started looking for jobs.

Yet, from those humble beginnings, I've achieved the lifestyle I dreamt of as a child. That dream included, but wasn't limited to, a highly rewarding and high-paying job that provided options and opportunities for my family. My career has been both challenging and rewarding, and this book details my truth. I share, in these pages, actual events that have occurred in my work life. These experiences became my teachers, and they have formed the basis of the lesson plans I've used to navigate my clients to greater success. Today, I share them with you in the hope that my lessons learned might help to guide you to your desired destination of a higher paying and more rewarding job.

Noble Servant Syndrome

Another motive for writing this book is my desire to free women from the "noble servant" syndrome. I run into this all too often. There's a cultural bias against women striving to earn more. This is particularly prevalent in spiritual communities, but it cuts across cultural, racial, and religious borders. This pernicious bias often shows up in subtle ways, such as through negative comments some religious acquaintances made when I left my full-time ministry to return to corporate America. Women are often encouraged to work in certain fields so they can be of service to others, even though the jobs barely pay a living wage. There exists this idea that it's somehow less noble to do a job that pays well, that you're greedy and materialistic if you're willing to work hard, be aggressive, and speak up for yourself in order to earn as much as you can and provide a nice life for your family.

Let me be clear. I do enjoy nice things. I also enjoy having the financial wherewithal to help a loved one in an emergency and to support charitable organizations when and how I choose to. If I didn't carefully manage my career and work to regularly increase my salary it might've been difficult for my family to afford a trip from Georgia to the Napa Valley, much less indulge in luxuries like balloon rides. I make no apologies for earning a high salary, nor do I apologize for the ways I choose to spend, save, share, or invest that money.

I'm here to assure you that there is nothing wrong with wanting to earn top dollar for the work you do every day. While money may not be the only important factor in the job you choose—it certainly isn't the only factor for me—it should be a significant part of your decision-making process when you choose your next position. There's nothing immoral, unladylike, or improper about wanting to be financially rewarded at the highest possible level for the job you do. I want you to know that you don't have to martyr yourself in a low-paying job in order to be fulfilled in your work. You can be of service every day and still earn enough money to pay your bills on time, to finance your children's extracurricular activities and college education, and to buy the luxuries you desire.

What's In It for You?

An attitude of continual learning and self-improvement is essential to building a flourishing career that can take you wherever you want to go in your professional life. Make time to read this book from cover to cover even if you already feel you are where you want to be. We can all improve, in any area, at any time. Even in your greatest strengths you may find one small thing you can recalibrate that can make a difference for you.

If you're deep in job searching, however, and need to find the right position as soon as possible, I encourage you to first get into the chapters that cover the next task you have to face. If you have an interview scheduled tomorrow, please jump to that section. Come back later and read the rest. Trust me. It all works together to give you the best possible preparation for a successful job search and consistent career growth.

Recalibrate is divided into three main sections: Check, Adjust, and Determine. Each section is quick to read and provides helpful navigation tools and techniques. There are fresh concepts and practical steps you can apply immediately. You'll also find Quick Recalibrations designed to help you apply specific and practical ways to get started today.

In section one, Check, I debunk the myths that may be keeping you from landing your dream job or increasing your salary. You'll focus on the work you need to do to get your mind right for a job search, and it all starts with understanding the unique value you bring to the marketplace. I also show you how to differentiate yourself from your peers and colleagues so you always have an answer when someone asks why you're the right person for a job.

Just as importantly, getting clarity on your professional worth will help you begin to shift your mindset so you can go about your job hunt with a new level of confidence. You'll also define the why behind your goals and identify what's important to you in a work environment and in a specific position so you can identify companies that meet your needs and decide which ones to target.

In the second section, Adjust, we tackle practical strategies for building your career. I share ways you can make specific recalibrations—some slight and some significant— to present yourself as the best candidate. You'll find suggestions for how to improve your resume, how to prepare for interviews of all kinds, what to do and what not to do during the interview process, and how to follow up. For those who don't necessarily want to leave their current employers, this section also includes direction on how to earn, ask for, and receive a raise or promotion.

In the final section, Determine, I share principles that will help you take all the mindset work and practical strategies and consistently use them to build the career you desire. This section reinforces the belief system I strive to help you adopt throughout this book, a view rooted in the knowledge that all things are possible.

It's my hope that each woman who reads this book, in part or in whole, will come away with a greater sense of her own value as an employee, a specific plan for how she can increase that value and make the most of it, and the confidence to do so.

"If you want something you've never had, you must be willing to do something you've never done." — Thomas Jefferson

Read something that made you think, 'I should try this?' WRITE it down here. Once you finish the book, come back to this Reflection page and begin to create your plan to incorporate it into your life.

_____

_____

_____

_____

_____

_____

_____

_____

_____

_____

_____

_____

Check

Recalibrate | verb | *to check and adjust by comparison to a standard; to determine and make corrections in.*

Check

I've coached clients with widely different levels of work experience and financial success, and no matter what they've accomplished or how challenging their goals, our work together always starts with a self-assessment. Through this process of checking in with themselves each person gets more clarity on what she really wants, why she wants it, and how she can achieve it.

I highly recommend you go through all the exercises in this section, whether you're currently in the market for a new job or not. The three-step process will help you grow in confidence and self-worth and open your mind to the many paths you can take to achieve what you want.

To start on your journey to career success, you need to:

1. Understand your unique value.
2. Overcome career-killing myths.
3. Envision the future you want and plan to achieve it.

Understand Your Unique Value

If you have even the slightest doubt about your ability to navigate the job market with confidence, land your dream job, and earn substantially more money than you make right now, you are selling yourself short. Once you understand your true value and your ability to increase that value, your future possibilities become limitless. The following exercise will help you do that.

Grab a pen and paper or open a document on your computer and create a list of your skills. Include the things you do every day in your job, software or applications you regularly use, leadership roles you've taken on, and projects you've worked on or headed. Jot down anything you've learned or accomplished outside your professional life, perhaps through volunteer work or hobbies. List any education or training you have, whether you use it at work or not. Include special skills or experiences, such as speaking multiple languages or having lived overseas for some time.

When you're done, look over your list. First, realize that there's no other person in the world whose list would be exactly the same as yours. Second, examine the items and decide which one or two can really separate you from the pack when it's time to look for a job. Again, it doesn't have to be directly related to your current work or the job you want. It just needs to add value or describe something wonderfully unique about you. If, for example, you run ultramarathons, an employer could see that as a sign that you have exceptional commitment and discipline, valuable qualities indeed.

If you find yourself struggling to identify your unique value, don't give up. Sometimes we take for granted the things that make us special. Ask someone who knows you well what comes to mind when they think of you, what they would come to you for advice about, or what they think makes you unique. I've yet to meet a person who couldn't complete this

> *Whether you realize it or not, there's something unique and valuable that only you can bring to the workplace.*

exercise successfully, and my clients consistently tell me it gives them a new level of confidence in their professional potential.

Until you're so convinced of your own unique value that you can rattle it off without thinking, you'll need to come back to this list. Return to it when you're feeling challenged in the pursuit of your dream job. Review it when you're revising your resume or preparing for an interview. Understanding what separates you from your peers is essential to helping employers see why they should choose you and to help you go after what you want without the fear of failure.

Overcome Career-Killing Myths

Recalibrating your mindset to prepare to go after your dream job requires you to take an honest look at the beliefs you hold. Our culture is inundated with false beliefs about how successful careers are made. These are the myths that keep people day after day dragging off to jobs they hate. These are the lies that keep you from landing your dream job or earning enough money to have the lifestyle you want.

As you read through these myths—and the truths that contradict them—reflect on what you actually believe about your ability to design the life and career you desire. Consider why you think that way and what that kind of thinking may have cost you.

It's time to fulfill your potential. Decide today to change your way of looking at your career. Start by assessing whether you have fallen prey to any of these myths and working to adjust your mindset to one that's always looking for opportunities and expecting to find them.

Myth: You have to be ruthless to survive in corporate America.

You see it in the movies all the time. The high-powered female executive wields her tongue like a sword. There's a slight chance she might be nice at home, but at the office she talks down to colleagues, demeans the people who work for her, and more or less alienates everyone around her. She is, to put it bluntly, a diva, and she usually ends up wealthy but lonely. Sitting in the theater audience, we're supposed to be convinced that her nastiness is both a blessing and a curse, at the same time the key to her success and the reason her employees fantasize about poisoning her coffee.

The kernel of truth in this myth is that taking charge of your career does require a certain amount of courage and even some toughness. However, the reality in most companies is that you'll have more influence when you win allies than when you create enemies. Being ruthless is not only unnecessary; it's counterproductive. Fully satisfying careers are built on a foundation of positive relationships, and you can't create those when coworkers resent you.

Myth: You have to compromise your values to succeed in corporate America.

Barbara was particularly concerned about this. In some of her self-assessment work she explained very clearly why she wanted to increase her income. She was determined to raise the standard of living for her two children, a goal to which most parents can relate. However, being a Christian, Barbara worried that she'd have to compromise her faith in order to succeed in the world of business. She felt torn between the desire to increase her income and the fear that it would require her to sell out to greed, backstabbing, or a willingness to lie and cheat.

Perhaps some people do get ahead by taking shortcuts or throwing coworkers under the bus. Sometimes the bad guys do seem to finish first, but the chickens always come home to roost, and whether we see it or not, those bad guys pay a price. Just think of the white collar criminals carted off in handcuffs while their prized possessions are auctioned off to the highest bidder. For every one of them there are thousands of people who have quietly achieved their success with their integrity intact. You can too.

Myth: To get ahead in business you have to be political.

Have you ever worked with an office kiss-up? Maybe she spent a little too much time in the boss's office. Maybe his disposition was too flawlessly positive or he went out of his way to socialize with his superiors outside of work. What about the annoying coworker who seemed to know just a little too much about what was going on behind the scenes? Any of those people could be accused of playing into office politics. And maybe they were. It's hard to know what anyone's real motives are.

Office politics are real, but the problem is that politics has gotten such a bad reputation we forget there's nothing inherently bad in being political. In its simplest form, it just means you seek and exercise power. Anytime a diverse body of human beings comes together to reach common goals there will always be conflicting priorities and differences of opinion.

> *Use your power and influence for good; being political can be one of your greatest strengths.*

Alliances will form, and you may have to choose a side. This only becomes a problem when the differences become toxic and people take on a "win at all costs" attitude. If it's happening where you work you can either rise above it, strive to improve the situation, or look for somewhere else to work. Use your power and your influence for good, and being political can be one of your greatest strengths.

Myth: You need 100% competency for a job before you apply for it.

This is a dangerous belief because you may never be able to check off every detail of the requirements for the job you really want. As a hiring manager and as a career coach, I've noticed that men tend not to care as much as women about having all the qualifications for a job. They'll happily apply for a position they're sort of qualified to do and come into the interview full of swagger and ready to go. Women, on the other hand, tend to shy away from applying for a job until they get a little more experience.

Obviously, I'm generalizing along gender lines, and there are plenty of exceptions to contradict those observations, but by and large, my experience bears them out. The good news is that it doesn't have to be that way. No, you shouldn't apply to be an emergency room doctor if you haven't gone to medical school, but the competencies you'll use in most environments tend to be more fluid and obtainable. If you're 80% qualified for your dream job, it's time you apply for it. You have the talent and intelligence to learn the other 20% on the job.

Myth: Full-time positions offer real security in a company.

For most of us, the days of joining a company at a young age and working there until we get the gold watch are over. However, many people still believe the greatest security can be found in holding a full-time position with a "solid" company. The recent recession reminded us of how quickly a seemingly stable job can disappear when employers are forced to go through layoffs. The kicker: in that climate, some companies choose to keep contractors while letting go of full-timers.

The wise professional knows the only real job security comes from making yourself incredibly valuable and distinguishing yourself from your peers. It doesn't matter how long you've worked for a company or in what capacity. You should position yourself so that you're the last one they want to let go, and even if you fall victim to a layoff, you're such an attractive candidate that other employers are clamoring to hire you. In other words, security with any one company, in a permanent, full-time position or otherwise, is a myth.

Myth: If you're really good at your job your career will grow on its own.

You show up to work on time every day, put your head down, and do everything that's expected of you. You even go above and beyond your job description because you believe a job worth doing is worth doing well. If that means staying late, you're willing to eat dinner at your desk. Of course, your boss will notice that you do more than your counterpart two cubicles over, and you'll be rewarded accordingly. Right?

Not likely. When you don't ask for more you rarely get more—and I'm not talking about the yearly 3% increase most people can expect to see in good economic times[1]. Think about it. Does that tiny increase make a material difference in your life? The way to reap your reward isn't just to work harder. You have to make sure people recognize your efforts and accomplishments. You have to document them, talk about them, and use them to ask for more money on your current job or the next one.

Myth: You should accept whatever offer you receive for a new job.

Anyone looking for a new job could consider themselves to be in a position of weakness. You're the one in need. They're the ones with all the power. You're hungry, and they have the bread. So you go in, and you do your dance, and you hope they

---

[1] Bean-Mellinger, Barbara. "The Average Salary Raise Percentage." Chron.com. Accessed December 13, 2015. http://work.chron.com/average-salary-raise-percentage-17983.html.

choose you, and when they do, you're so grateful to be at the table, that yes, you're happy to take the crumbs.

No, ma'am. Whether you've been laid off or fired, haven't worked in a decade, or still have a job to go to every day, you have value. Once you identify what makes you a unique candidate and understand how to make the most of that value in the job market you'll see that you absolutely do not have to settle. When you know your worth and demonstrate it to others, you can command the salary you deserve.

Envision the Future You Want and Plan to Achieve It

One of my favorite career-coaching tools is the Career Vision Plan worksheet. It's designed to help you understand what's important to you, why you want it, and how you'll get it. Your vision statement will help you decide what steps to take next and stay focused in the face of challenges. You can find a downloadable copy of the Career Vision Plan Worksheet at YvetteGavin.com

At the top of the worksheet you'll see a space to write your vision statement. This will be the very last thing you fill in if you're uncertain about what you really want to do. You'll create it based on what you learn about yourself while you fill in the rest of the worksheet. Start with the questions at the bottom. They'll give you clarity on what you really want. Use that information to fill in your goals, and lastly, to create your vision statement. If you are certain about your vision, go ahead and write your vision statement.

What is most important to you?

In this section list the things that matter most in your life. Use the extra space to the right if you need more room, but you want to capture your core values here. This might include your health, your faith, or your marriage or other relationships. Don't just focus on your career. These priorities are the reasons why you're willing to work hard for what you want. Keep them at the front of your mind when it's time to take risks and stretch yourself to achieve big goals.

What is non-negotiable?

List what you must have in your life and career. If you know you can't work for your current company for much longer, for example, then finding a new company to work for rather than trying to get a promotion where you are is non-negotiable.

What is the greatest threat to achieving your vision?

What do you need to change about your mindset, your behavior, or your situation in order to achieve your goals? A lack of confidence, a habit of associating with the wrong people, and a habit of tardiness would all fit here. These are things you will determine to correct.

How will you manage conflicts?

We all have conflicts in the things we want to achieve. If you're responsible for picking your kids up from school every day but you really need to participate in a training program offered in the afternoons, you'll need to figure out how to manage that or find an alternative.

How will you manage your time in order to achieve your goals?

Many people struggle to take action because they don't manage their time well. List the ways you'll overcome any challenges in this area. For example, you might need to get up an hour earlier every day to spend time researching companies or revising your resume.

Short-Term Goals.

In this section you'll list the things you want to accomplish within the next six months. This can include anything from revising your resume to joining a professional networking group or landing a job that finally lets you reach six figures.

Long-term Goals.

Anything you believe will take you more than six months to achieve will go in this section. This might include launching a business, completing a degree, or buying a new home. Big goals with lots of steps are likely to fit in this category.

Developmental Activities.

These are the specific things you'll need to achieve your goal. This includes things such as organizational skills, a system for your research, better time management, or improved focus.

Career Vision Statement.

This short sentence defines who you are—or are working to become—professionally. Write it in the present tense so you can start to envision it as your reality now. Your vision statement can be as simple as, "I am a highly-valued and highly-paid Quality Assurance Director." In that case I would challenge you to understand what that title means to you. Which of your values is it fulfilling? Is your vision about the title of director, or is it about a certain income or level of responsibility? Be sure you're clear about what you really want to achieve.

If you have trouble figuring out what your vision for your career really is, ask yourself a few more questions. What is your passion? What are your greatest skills? What job would you be willing to do even if you didn't get paid to do it? You may be struggling to create your vision because you don't believe you can have what you want. For the time being, allow yourself complete freedom in answering these questions. You can deal with how you can have what you want after you're completely clear on what that is.

Once you've worked through the exercises in this section you should be clear about the unique value you bring to the job market. You should have begun to recalibrate your thinking to undo any limiting beliefs you've held about your career. And now you have a vision for where you want to go. In the next section you'll get into the practical details of how to position yourself for your dream job and go after it with confidence.

"If you want something you've never had, you must be willing to do something you've never done." — Thomas Jefferson

Read something that made you think, 'I should try this?' WRITE it down here. Once you finish the book, come back to this Reflection page and begin to create your plan to incorporate it into your life.

_____

_____

_____

_____

_____

_____

_____

_____

_____

_____

_____

_____

Adjust

Recalibrate | verb | *to check and adjust by comparison to a standard; to determine and make corrections in.*

Adjust

Position Yourself for Promotions and Raises

If you like working for your current company but you know you should be advancing faster and earning more, take a look at the opportunities where you are. You might be able to find what you're looking for without jumping ship. Even if there's not a new position currently available you can prepare yourself now to make a case for a significant salary increase in the job you have today, and then you can apply for the right position when it opens.

Make the Most of Your Current Position

1. Keep a running list of your accomplishments.
2. Practice the "subtle self-promote."
3. Speak up about your professional goals.
4. Protect your money.
5. Always be the problem-solver.
6. Connect, especially with your boss.
7. Stay true to your value system.
8. Ask for the money.

Keep a Running List of Your Accomplishments

No one knows your work better, or cares more about it, than you do. You never want to sit down at your computer at the last minute the day before an evaluation and rack your brain to figure out exactly what you've achieved. Get started on a list of your professional accomplishments today, and update it often.

Your list should include as many achievements as you can come up with, and the more you can quantify them the greater impact they'll have. If you helped a team member improve his performance, note exactly what you did and the percentage of improvement. If you completed a project early, detail how many days you shaved off the deadline and how much money you saved the company by finishing early. When you tie your successes to the bottom line you'll shine as a star team member, someone who provides value and has the potential to contribute to the company at a higher level.

Practice the Subtle Self-Promote

Bragging without ceasing about what you've done is a sure way to turn people off and even make a few enemies. However, you do need to let your boss and other influential people know you're making things happen. When you receive an email thanking you for a job well done or congratulating you on your latest achievement, reply with a thank you and copy your boss on the email exchange.

No matter how hard you work or what your boss observes, it's always good to have direct feedback from other team members or different departments to add to the information by which your performance will be evaluated. Allow other people to do your bragging for you and make sure you leave the kind of impression that makes them rave about you when your name comes up.

In addition, you should strive to be the kind of person who brags about the accomplishments of others, whether you're deserving of some of the credit or not. When you do assist a teammate with her work let your boss know by bragging about her first. Celebrate how quickly the teammate picked up the concept you explained to her. In that conversation, you're not only demonstrating that you have the generosity to promote coworkers, you're also shining a spotlight on your own contribution to your colleague's success while giving her the credit she should get.

Speak Up About Your Professional Goals

You work hard, show up on time, stay late, and exceed expectations day after day. None of that necessarily means you're looking to advance to a better position. You can't expect your boss or anyone else to guess that you don't plan to stay in your current role until you retire.

It may seem common sense to you, but not everyone wants to take on more responsibility or greater challenges at work. Some people are just happy to do their job and collect their paycheck every two weeks. If that's not you, you need to speak up and make it clear to the people in charge that you plan to go after something more.

Protect Your Money

When I was a young creative director, writing copy and putting my early journalism training to good use, I prided myself on making sure my content was always on point. It paid off. At a year-end review my manager had nothing but positive comments, except for one thing. She pointed out some copy I'd written months earlier and told me that a particular word I'd chosen to use wasn't even a word in that context.

I was shocked, and I was sure the mistake would take a few percentage points off the merit increase I was expecting to get. It certainly would've been better for me if she hadn't waited until the review to point out my mistake, and I told her as much. Then I went out and did my own research on the issue.

Because I grew up in a small country town and didn't always have the kind of vocabulary I thought a writer from a big city would have, I was incredibly careful to put forth the best possible copywriting. I even made a habit of calling university grammar hotlines when I had any doubts about my work. This time, I took the issue my manager pointed out to the hotline, but I skipped over the graduate students to run my question by the professors.

After speaking with two different English experts, both of whom confirmed that my usage of the word was perfectly correct, I went back to my manager. My purpose wasn't to say, "I told you so." My purpose was to protect my money.

I explained to her what I'd discovered and cited my sources. I was careful to frame the conversation around my desire to learn so I wouldn't make the same mistake again rather than presenting it as challenging her opinion. Her face turned red as she listened to my explanation and then apologized to me.

When you mess up, you have to take responsibility, do your best to rectify the mistake, and demonstrate what you've learned from the challenge. However, you don't have to sit back and accept blame for something that's not your fault. It may seem to be no big deal at the moment. Maybe you don't want to rock the boat. But that mistake, big or small, can come back to haunt you when it's time for your evaluation or when you're applying for a promotion or asking for a raise. When you're being erroneously blamed for something, respectfully clarify what happened and point out why you're not deserving of a slap on the wrist.

Always Be the Problem-Solver

In one of my positions with a content distributor, I oversaw a team of twenty-three employees. One day a team member approached me to say she didn't feel comfortable viewing the adult content she was required to watch as part of her quality assurance work. I completely understood and wanted to help her find a way to do her job without compromising her morals.

When I went to my boss to discuss the employee's concerns, he responded by telling me that was just the way things were done in our department. While it wasn't the response I'd hoped for, I didn't believe he had any bad intentions. In fact, I was certain he viewed it as a job requirement that couldn't be changed.

Once I realized his position on the subject I knew I couldn't come back to him without a workable solution. It wouldn't do me or my team members any good for me to make a big deal out of it without offering a viable alternative. I did some research. And as I dug into the matter I identified potential risks the policy created for our company.

Sure, I'd found potential problems, but I still didn't have the solution. So I delved into the process and discovered that the actual material our team members viewed was irrelevant to maintaining quality assurance for content delivery. The real responsibility lay in making sure the technology worked properly, and there were other ways to do that. In the end, I was able to present a workable solution using the same technology to view more acceptable material and satisfy my employee, my boss, and the company's need.

There will be occasions when you notice opportunities for improvement in department processes, company policies, or your work environment. You should bring those things to your boss's attention, but no one likes a complainer. Do your research. Brainstorm. Consider the problem from different angles, and always focus on the company's motivation. Find a way to help your boss achieve his or her goals. Then, when you set forth your concerns you can also lay out your proposed solutions. Even if no one follows through on your plan, you demonstrate that you're a proactive, concerned team player.

Connect, Especially with Your Boss

Early in my career I was convinced that if I just kept my head down, worked hard, and produced quality work, over time I'd reap the benefits with maxed-out bonuses, raises, and consistent promotions. I found out just how wrong I was when a co-worker, who was much more of a squeaky wheel than I'd ever been, shared her annual merit increase with me.

You guessed it. They gave her more money than they gave me.

My performance review was excellent. There wasn't one negative thing in there. Even though I'd been training co-workers and going above and beyond my job duties, my increase didn't measure up to what I was putting in. I got a certificate for teamwork, but no major increase in pay. When I asked about it my boss told me because I was quiet at work everyone assumed I was content with where I was and what I earned.

In another position, my manager actually pulled me aside and told me I wasn't giving her enough facetime to build a relationship with her. Even though I was leading and directing the team and taking on added responsibilities so she could focus on other things, that wasn't enough. She explained to me that people who make the effort to connect with the boss are much more likely to be treated with favor.

After both incidents, I looked around and realized that the people getting promotions were those who had made connections with key people. I didn't want to waste time kissing up. I didn't want to play games or get involved in "office politics," but I learned that you don't have to play games to effectively network on the job.

Of course, you should be respectful of everyone and take the time to greet whomever you come across at the office. From the custodians and cafeteria workers to the CEO, everyone should be happy to see you coming. But too many people are afraid to reach out and say hello to senior leaders. Recalibrate your thinking in this area and vow not to be the one who misses out on job opportunities because she's afraid to connect with office influencers.

When you cross paths with an influential person take a moment to introduce yourself and inquire about her day. You can easily assess when she's busy and wrap the conversation quickly, but a simple greeting on a regular basis can go a long way to making her aware of who you are and how you contribute to the company.

Connect with your boss by asking about his weekend, inquiring about his children, congratulating him on the successful completion of a project, or just poking your head into his office to say hello. You don't want to make a pest of yourself and you can't force a relationship. However, you can show yourself to be approachable and engaged by asking tasteful questions. Find a common ground to talk about so your boss will recognize you're not just another cog in the machine. If you want to be his peer, or even his boss at some point, you'll need him and others to see you as someone they could easily talk to, collaborate with, and turn to for help.

Stay True to Your Value System

Years ago, when I held a creative director position that required me to entertain visiting clients, I was asked to do something that challenged my personal values. I actually enjoyed taking clients out to four-star restaurants, the theater, and various professional sporting events. That is, I enjoyed it until one client asked me to book a female companion for him.

I'm from Greenville, Georgia, population 865[2]. Yes, I was a bit naïve, but I had no idea what he wanted me to do. When I asked, my boss explained that the client expected me to arrange for a stripper to keep him company on his visit.

"This isn't about your personal values," she said. "You need to do it."

What consenting adults do is their business, but hiring a woman to entertain my client in such a way went against what I believe to be right. It absolutely was about my personal values, and I respectfully declined to do it. My boss found someone else who had no problem handling it, and I was off the hook.

I have to admit I was concerned my refusal to participate in something I found immoral and distasteful would hurt me when it came time for my annual evaluation, but surprisingly, the subject didn't even come up. I'm sure part of the reason was that the company could face a human resources issue for even asking me to do something like that. But I was also producing in a big way for the client and for my employer. Everyone was happy with the results I was getting, and in the end, that was all that mattered.

There may be times when taking a stand like that actually hurts your job progress, but it's never worth selling your soul to get what you want. Stay true to what you believe to be right.

Ask For the Money

You have not because you ask not. This is one my favorite bible verses, and it applies to the majority of working people who aren't earning what they deserve. Most people never bother to ask for a raise. That's a shame because asking works. A 2014 survey by Payscale, a company that produces compensation models, found that 44% of people who ask for a raise will get it. That's a risk worth taking. Unfortunately, only 44% of men and 42% of women will ever ask.

---

[2] "Greenville, Georgia." (GA 30222) Profile: Population, Maps, Real Estate, Averages, Homes, Statistics, Relocation, Travel, Jobs, Hospitals, Schools, Crime, Moving, Houses, News, Sex Offenders. Accessed December 13, 2015. http://www.city-data.com/city/Greenville-Georgia.html.

It's not unusual to find yourself underpaid in your position. Your employer is in business to make a profit. They'll usually be happy to pay you as little as you're willing to accept to get you to do your job, so it's up to you to do what you can to maximize your salary.

Earlier I mentioned a time when I discovered a coworker, who did less but spoke up more, was earning more money than me. I was so young in my career I didn't really understand how these things worked and I took it personally that all my effort was being overlooked. On my way home from picking up my son from daycare that day, I passed the office and noticed my boss's car still there. Upset over my insufficient raise, I swung into the parking lot, grabbed the baby out of his car seat, and went in to talk to her.

I was more emotional than I should've been for that conversation, but I had my "why" sitting quietly next to me, and I let my boss know I wasn't happy with my merit increase, given how much work I was putting in and the results I was getting for the company. It wasn't fair, I told her.

"Yvette," she told me, "life is not fair."

Ouch! She didn't validate me at all, and I ended up in tears. It was a hard way to learn the lesson that being great at what you do usually isn't enough. Although I didn't go about it in the best way, I eventually got a significant merit increase and later a promotion on that job. I do not advise anyone to take their child to a meeting with the boss, but if I'd never asked for more money I'm quite sure I'd have gone year after year receiving minimal merit increases and few promotions.

When you keep track of your accomplishments and quantify them where you can, you'll have the evidence to support your argument that you should be paid more. Use good judgment and decide if the time is right to ask for the money. (If the company is going through layoffs, you might want to reconsider.) Schedule some time to talk to your boss about opportunities for growth. Approach her with a positive attitude and share with her why you believe you're deserving of either a raise or a promotion with a raise. Don't treat this as an adversarial relationship. A wise boss will want to keep her best employees satisfied, so expect to work together on this.

If you don't get what you want, inquire as to what else you need to do to earn it. If the response is reasonable, try to work within those parameters. If not, it may be time to start looking for other opportunities. Many people find that changing companies is the fastest way to get significant income increases.

Quick Recalibration

⊕ Sit down today and update or create your list of accomplishments in your current position. Make sure you save this document where you can access it quickly.

Your Door-Opening Resume

Sometimes advancement within your company either isn't an option or isn't the right option for you. It's time to start looking for a new job, and that means polishing your resume. "Send me your resume," is the response I hear most often when seeking new positions for myself. It's also my go-to request when job-seekers reach out to me in their search. Why? Because the resume provides a quick assessment of the applicant's skills, experiences, and overall work background.

The resume has become the measuring stick by which human resources recruiters and hiring managers determine if it's worth the employer's time to invest in a conversation with an applicant. Like it or not, that's how people who have the power to hire you are using resumes. Your resume will either open or close the door on your career opportunities.

You're probably already aware that you need a resume for your job search, but most people fail to realize how you can drastically increase your appeal as a job candidate when you spend a little extra time making your resume really sing your praises. In many instances, small tweaks can mean the difference between being overlooked or pushed aside and getting a phone call to schedule an interview. Regardless of how long or short your work history, your resume needs to be easy to read, properly formatted, and filled with the kind of details that grab a recruiter's attention, and ultimately, the attention of the hiring manager.

> *The resume opens the door for a conversation. The interview lands the job.*

Few documents you draft will have as much impact on your career, so it would be foolish not to give it the proper time and attention. But don't be confused. The most important thing to know about your resume is that it will not get you a job. That's not its purpose. As a hiring manager, I would never make someone an offer based solely on a piece of paper that summarizes her skills and work experience. Of course, you still have work to do after you perfect your resume. Just keep in mind that this is an incredibly important part of your job search. It's how you'll introduce yourself to the gatekeepers who stand between you and your dream job.

Unless you have a personal referral from someone within the company, your resume is the one thing that lets decision-makers know you exist and upon which they will determine whether you are ready, willing, and able to do the job. It creates the first impression—good or bad—that the recruiter, human resources representative, or hiring manager has of you. Even if a friend or colleague successfully connects you with a hiring manager, eventually you'll be asked to provide a resume. It's just a part of the process.

Your resume has one purpose: to land you the interview. It's the golden key that opens the door for a conversation about a potential position. Let's make it as effective at its job as it can be.

Elements of an Effective Resume:

1. Contact Information
2. Executive Summary
3. Technical Skills
4. Professional Experience
5. Intellectual Property
6. Education
7. Professional Training and Certification
8. Awards and Volunteer Activities
9. Professional Memberships

Now, don't panic as you read that list. Depending on where you are on your career path, you may not have all those elements under your belt just yet. If not, you'll be relieved to know they're not all required for every position and many of them are easy to acquire even when you're just getting started. Whatever attributes you bring to the table, this chapter will coach you to showcase them in the best possible way. You need to position your assets to catch the interest of decision-makers, and I'll show you how to do it.

Notice that I didn't include references on this list of resume essentials. While many applicants put them on their resumes, they don't belong there. References should only be sent to a potential employer after they're requested.

Let's dive into the resume essentials.

Contact Information

I recently met an intelligent, talented, hard-working young woman who had just started medical school. She shared with me that the name I knew her by had originally been her middle name, but her high school counselor had advised her that if she wished to succeed in a competitive field such as medicine, she should change her first name. It was just too ethnic, the counselor warned, for anyone to take seriously. This young lady took the counselor's advice and legally switched her first and middle names. She was convinced the less conventional first name she'd been given at birth would be an obstacle when she applied to schools and for jobs, and she wanted to do what she could to smooth her path to success.

A legal name-change is clearly an extreme case, and we could have an endless debate about the appropriateness of a counselor doling out that kind of advice. But truth is, names do matter. A 2003 study by the National Bureau of Economic Research determined that with all things being equal, fictitious applicants with "white-sounding names" were 50% more likely to be called for initial interviews than were applicants with "African American-sounding names."[3]

People, not machines, are reviewing your resume, and we all come with our own biases. You really want the person reading your resume to choose you for an interview before she makes judgments based on conscious or unconscious biases she might hold against certain ethnic groups. Whether or not you'll go so far as to alter your name in some way is a very personal choice. However, it's worth being aware of the potential bias so you can make an informed decision.

Making it easy for recruiters and employers to get in touch with you by providing all your contact information might seem to be common sense, but it can be a bit tricky in certain circumstances. It might surprise you that these days I'm not a huge fan of including your mailing address on your resume, for two reasons. First, it's pretty rare for anyone to contact you about a job via snail mail. Second, including your physical address can sometimes work against you.

Let's say you live in Connecticut, but you're applying for jobs in Georgia. A human resources representative or hiring manager could look at your resume and immediately see potential relocation expenses. Why should they consider you when there are perfectly good candidates who won't require thousands of extra dollars to take the job? Your first goal should be to sell them on you as the perfect candidate without clouding the conversation with distractions, such as what it will take for you to accept the job and make the move. If you choose to put an out-of-state address on your resume, consider stating in a cover letter your plans for relocating.

[3] Bertrand, Marianne, and Sendhil Mullainathan. "ARE EMILY AND GREG MORE EMPLOYABLE THAN LAKISHA AND JAMAL? A FIELD EXPERIMENT ON LABOR MARKET DISCRIMINATION." NATIONAL BUREAU OF ECONOMIC RESEARCH. July 1, 2003. Accessed December 13, 2015. http://www.nber.org/papers/w9873.pdf.

"But," you say, "I'm looking for a job in my own city." Well, don't get too comfortable with adding your street address to your resume. I've seen hiring managers reject a candidate because the manager decided the commute would be too long for the candidate. A decision-maker could also be biased against or in favor of certain neighborhoods in your city, something that's impossible to predict. You still may choose to share your physical address, but consider those potential issues when you're deciding.

While home address is optional, you should always put your phone number on your resume. In the cellphone age, an out-of-state area code isn't likely to lock you out of a job because employers recognize that many people keep cellphone numbers from cities where they lived when they started their cell service.

Unless they're specifically required for the job you're seeking, do not include your social media contacts on your resume. Yes, it shows that you have a millennial mindset and you're up on the latest social media platforms, but your online profiles and activity can reveal way too much about you at this point in the process.

With a click of the mouse, potential employers will immediately draw conclusions about your race and ethnicity, your approximate age, and even your religion or sexuality. They may view photos of you doing things that seem harmless to you, but which completely turn off a hiring manager or recruiter. For instance, you could have a seemingly innocent photo of yourself having dinner with a glass of wine on the table. A decision-maker who has a bias against people who consume alcohol could use that to eliminate you from the hiring process. You don't want to be judged on superficial things when you haven't even had a chance to show how great you are for this position.

If your LinkedIn profile is poorly composed, your photo is unprofessional, or you display questionable behavior or anything that might be personally offensive to a decision-maker on any social media account, you could cheat yourself out of an opportunity. A recruiter or hiring manager might take the time to search for you on social media platforms, so they should always represent you well, but you don't need to lead them there so early in the process. Leave social media accounts off your resume.

Your email address must appear in your contact information, but make sure it's not one that might cause a negative reaction. I once reviewed the resume of a woman who was incredibly sharp and skilled at her job. Let's call her Lucy. The first thing I noticed was that her email address was hotlucy@emailservice.com. That's just not acceptable for a professional job search. If your email address is something you thought was funny, or sexy, or cute, and you don't want to change it, create a second email account with a simple, professional name you can use for your job search.

Include your name, email address, and phone number on all pages of your resume. After the first page, put that contact information in the header or footer.

Executive Summary

The executive summary is a short paragraph that details the high-level skills you bring to the table and defines what type of position you're seeking. It focuses on the elements you want to highlight, your relevant professional strengths. This is your chance to shape your professional persona in the way you want hiring managers and recruiters to see it.

As I write this, I currently work in a Quality Assurance (QA) leadership capacity, but I'm also an accomplished Information Technology (IT) management resource who has led business analysts, project managers, and technical writers. Rather than limit myself to QA positions, I want to be recognized for my leadership experience and ability. Instead of writing about QA in my executive summary, I describe my "proven ability in building high-performance onshore and offshore teams." Immediately, recruiters see I can handle responsibility for diverse team dynamics. They focus on my leadership ability, and I'm not pigeonholed as someone who only does quality assurance.

If you're trying to move into a management position for the first time, use this section to highlight your leadership experience. If you've been a team lead or taken responsibility for a project, note it here. You don't have to wear an official title as manager to call yourself a leader. If you've trained people, you can take credit for that even though you've never held an official position as a corporate trainer. When describing your abilities, don't limit yourself to the job titles you've held.

Professional Strengths

In this list you want to make sure you use the language of the industry in which you want to work and the role you want to fill. Pay attention. This is critical. Recruiters search job sites using keywords in much the same way you use a major search engine. If those industry buzzwords aren't on your resume, you'll never get a phone call because your resume will never show up for recruiters.

Do your own search for job descriptions that fit what you're looking for and make a list of ten common keywords to include in your professional strengths. In my case, I need to use phrases such as "change management," "product management," and "organizational development." These are key phrases that are often used in the kind of jobs I'd seek.

From a hiring perspective, I can tell you that we often choose people who already have industry experience. Retail people like to hire retail people. Telecomm looks for telecomm. I don't want to have to dig through resumes and try to guess whether a candidate has relevant experience. I'll ask about it in an interview, but if I don't know about it you might not get that far. Using industry vocabulary sends the message that you're familiar with and experienced in the field.

If you want to cross into a new industry, don't give up. Focus on leveraging the experience you have instead of the industries you've worked in. Years ago I wanted to transition from my career as a journalist and editor, which I loved but which paid little, to the technical side of business where I could earn significantly higher salaries. I didn't have a lot of technical ability or experience at the time, but I applied for and got a technical writing position. I leveraged the strength of my written communication skills to move into IT where I wanted to be.

Professional Experience

Create a detailed account of where you've worked, in what role, and when. Start with your current job and work your way backward. I generally go back about ten years in listing my experience. For most recruiters the older jobs will be less impressive or less relevant, so you don't want to lead with them. However, if you're making a career change later in life and the earlier experience is most relevant you should consider including it.

The name of the company you've worked for, along with the city and state where it's located, can sometimes give you a leg up. Decision-makers sometimes judge candidates based on whether their previous company is large or small, established or a start-up, or their own sole venture. We all have biases about certain recognizable companies as well. Coca-Cola is a name that typically draws a positive response. On the other end of the spectrum, there are some companies whose names raise an immediate red flag. If the company has a bad reputation, I'll ask the candidate to address some of the issues I've heard about—not because I want some dirt on the company—I want to see if the candidate can discuss a negative experience with grace.

Start with the specific department you worked for and the title of the position you held and include the years you served in each role. As a hiring manager, this gives me a good indication of how long I can expect you to stay in the position I'm trying to fill. It also lets me draw conclusions about how strong your skills are. If you only worked as a business analyst for one year, for example, it would be reasonable to conclude that your skill in that area isn't as strong as that of someone who held a similar role for three years.

Under each position, write a few sentences describing your most notable and relevant accomplishments. The more measurable these are in terms of percentages, dollars, or other statistics, the more they'll communicate about your performance. This is your chance to brag about what you've achieved. If you've been keeping a list of your professional accomplishments—and you should be—this will be fairly easy to do.

If you have gaps in your professional experience, you're certainly not alone. Many people have been out of the work force for periods of time for a wide variety of reasons. The important thing is that you address those gaps on your resume. Don't just ignore them. Significant time out of work won't go unnoticed.

It's always best to have some productive experience you can list for a given time period. If you volunteered in some capacity during a period of unemployment, list the volunteer work where you'd otherwise have a gap. You do not have to spell out that it was a non-compensated position. Describe what you did and leave out the fact that you weren't paid for it. If you went back to college or worked on a certification during that time, outline relevant course work or internships.

That said, if you face a period of unemployment in the future, make sure you do something to fill that gap. Volunteer with an organization that allows you to use and continue to develop your professional skills. Take continuing education classes. Go get that certification you always wanted but never had time to complete. That way you'll be prepared when it's time to update your resume. As an added benefit, getting out and doing regular volunteer work or taking classes can prevent you from sliding into the depression many people face when the job hunt lasts longer than expected. Volunteering or going to school can also help you meet people who can tell you about paying job opportunities. Use this time to build your network.

If you worked in an unconventional area such as ministry, use your judgment to decide, case by case, whether or not to include it on your resume when looking for a corporate position. At one point in my career, I left a job with a major airline to go into full-time ministry for two years. When I decided to reenter the work force I listed that experience on my resume, but now I tend to leave it off. If it becomes clear that I'm talking to a person of faith during an interview, I can bring up my ministry work. Otherwise, there's a chance it might be judged the wrong way. Fortunately, I did other things during that time period that I can list as professional experience, such as writing and publishing my first book.

A word of warning: It can be tempting to pad your resume with made-up experience, but that's a career-killing mistake. Inevitably, you'll get to the interview and find your answers can't support the exaggerations or outright lies. In addition, you never know when someone who is acquainted with you will see your resume and recognize fabrications. The world is smaller than you might think.

When a former co-worker sent me her resume to see if I could help her get a job with my employer, I was happy to do what I could to aid her in her job search. Unfortunately, I noticed that her resume listed her as a manager in the company where we once worked together. I knew that wasn't true because she'd reported to me during the time she claimed to hold the manager position. I was the manager! Clearly I couldn't move forward with helping her. That would mean I was co-signing her lie, and I wasn't willing to risk my career or compromise my integrity.

Even if you're luckier than she was and you manage to get through the interview process and land the job based on falsehoods, you'll still have to figure out how to keep the position and deliver on skills and knowledge you don't actually have. I once watched a friend land the journalism job she wanted by submitting copy written by someone else. Because she couldn't produce that quality of work for herself, she was quickly fired.

Lastly, keep in mind that all major companies will do a background check which includes verifying the employment history you've outlined on your job application and your resume.

Technical Skills

Most people shy away from including technical skills on their resumes unless they have 100% competency in those areas. I used to think I couldn't claim a technical skill unless I'd fully mastered it, but I learned that's a myth that can cost you the job you want. Don't sell yourself short. If you've worked with a particular software application or other tools and technologies relevant to the position you're applying for, include them all in this section of your resume. If the question of your level of competency comes up in the interview, you can address it by being honest about your skillset and asking for clarification on how much mastery of that particular technology is required for the position. Since you won't apply for a job that has technical requirements that are completely out of your reach, it shouldn't be an issue.

In one situation, I really wanted a job that called for more experience with a particular layout software tool than I had at the time. In that case, my husband went out and bought me a manual and I taught myself enough to get through the interview, land the job, and successfully handle my new responsibilities. It's okay to stretch, as long as you can actually do the job. List all the software, tools, and technologies with which you have a working familiarity.

Intellectual Property

Have you written a book, created an audio or video recording of a speech you gave, or developed an app? Do you hold any patents? These are accomplishments you should list in the "intellectual property" section of your resume. They don't have to be directly tied to the job you're trying to land. You're looking for something to help you stand out among a sea of qualified applicants, and this could be it.

Education

Coaching clients often ask me where they should put the "Education" section on their resumes. Should it go on the first page or the last page? Well, it depends. If you're been out of college for a long time and have years of work experience, add your educational summary on the last page. However, if you've recently graduated from college or a professional program and don't have a deep employment history, put your education on the first page. In that case, there are ways to make the most of this section of your resume so it can lift you above scores of applicants who've just finished their formal education and don't have much more to say about themselves than, "I have a degree."

If you have a very strong GPA, and by that I mean a 3.7 to 4.0, or if you graduated with honors, include those accomplishments here to set you apart from other applicants. While a 3.5 GPA is certainly something to be proud of, it's not uncommon, so I wouldn't bother to list it. Don't worry if you weren't that straight-A student. There are some other things you can highlight here

I was part of a panel that interviewed a candidate who noted on her resume that she was captain of her basketball team at a prestigious university. We immediately saw her potential to be a leader because she'd already successfully taken on a leadership role that required her to make decisions under pressure, motivate a team, and handle conflict.

Anything you did during your school years that shows leadership, teamwork, innovation, initiative, or academic excellence should be recorded here. Foreign travel, such as study abroad and exchange programs, can position you as a candidate with a broader worldview, so include that too.

Some experts will disagree, but I don't recommend mentioning your membership in fraternities or sororities, with the exception of honor societies that fall into this category. Every one of those organizations has loyal members and supporters, but there are also many people who may consider your organization a rival or simply associate it with negative experiences. Leave your Greek affiliation off your resume, but if you notice your interviewer has an office filled with your sorority's paraphernalia it might be worth mentioning the commonality the two of you share. It could be a point of connection that works in your favor.

Professional Training and Certification

Professional training and certification can freshen a resume for some of us who have been out of school for a while. List any recent training or certification you've gotten to make it clear that your knowledge and skills are current and relevant. This ongoing professional development demonstrates your commitment to your career and your willingness to learn new things.

Awards and Volunteer Activities

Right now volunteer work gets a lot of buzz among hiring decision-makers. We're looking for service on a candidate's resume. There will be times when your volunteer work will not only make you stand out, but also help the hiring manager connect to you because he or she has a similar interest or an affinity for the cause. Sharing your volunteer work shows employers you care about being part of something bigger than yourself. Listing various awards you've received says to employers that you're a high-achiever in various aspects of your life.

Professional Memberships

If you don't belong to any relevant professional organizations, I suggest you find one to join now. For a relatively small investment of time and money, you'll benefit in numerous ways. Participating in professional organizations demonstrates the importance you place on staying up-to-date on your industry and engaged with others in your profession. It lets employers know you take your career seriously. It also provides networking contacts outside your own company so when you're in the job market you'll have many more allies who can point you to opportunities.

Where to Submit Your Resume

Before you jump to upload your resume, make sure the format can be scanned and will still be easy to read. You can't expect recruiters to fight their way through a messy, cramped, hard-to-read document. If they can't hone in on the important points, they'll quickly move on to the next candidate. During a 2015 technical summit held at Cox Communications, Cox recruiters shared that they only spend two or three minutes reviewing a resume before they make a decision to exclude or include the candidate. Keep that in mind and make yours easy to say yes to.

After you've properly formatted your resume, have at least one other person proofread it. It's easy to miss your own mistakes, and spelling and grammar checks won't catch everything. As unfair as it may seem, a single glaring error could cost you the job. According to a 2012 survey by CareerBuilder, 61% of recruiters will dismiss your resume if they find typos on it.[4] Don't blow your chance to land your dream job over a misspelled word or punctuation error.

Once your resume is proofed to perfection and ready to go, you need to think beyond the major online job boards. There are job boards dedicated to specific industries and professions and to various audiences. They exist for everything from tech jobs to retail, beauty, healthcare, financial services, culinary arts, advertising, and more. Some job boards specifically target recent college graduates or other demographics. Do your research and find out which ones are a good match for you.

I also highly recommend Indeed.com. This site scours the Internet and brings back all the posted jobs that match your description. Of course, there are new services popping up all the time, so keep an eye on what's out there. Don't forget about LinkedIn. Although I don't recommend putting your LinkedIn information on your resume, I do recommend you have a LinkedIn page and use the site for job leads.

But don't stop there. Talk to your happily employed friends about their employers and do some online research on the best places to work in your industry. Make a list of five to ten companies where you'd love to work. Go directly to those targeted companies' job boards and apply for positions that would be a good match for you. If you don't see a job you want right now, submit your resume anyway. Most companies will accept resumes through their website even when you're not applying for a particular job. Many positions never make it to the boards, but the company will go to its database of resumes to find candidates. You may get a call for a job you never knew existed.

---

[4] "Thirty-six Percent of Employers Plan to Hire Full-Time, Permanent Employees in the New Year, CareerBuilder's Annual Forecast Finds - CareerBuilder." July 11, 2012. Accessed December 13, 2015. http://www.careerbuilder.com/share/aboutus/pressreleasesdetail.aspx?sd=7/11/2012&id=pr707&ed=12/31/2012

Job board listings aren't always updated in a timely manner either. A position could already be filled by the time you submit your resume. Other than an email acknowledging your submission has been received, don't expect to hear from a company unless and until they want to talk to you about an opening.

If you have a relationship with someone employed by a company where you're interested in working, you can ask if he or she would be willing to submit your resume on your behalf. As hiring managers, we typically give careful consideration to in-house referrals. But be aware that you're asking this person to vouch for you, and if this friend agrees, it's your responsibility to put your best foot forward, from your resume to the interviews and beyond. Everything you do reflects on the one who recommended you. It's a big favor that shouldn't be taken lightly.

When Barbara, the coaching client I helped to increase her income over 50%, sent our revised version of her resume to a colleague she'd asked to refer her for a position in the past, he was pleasantly surprised by the improvements. So much so, that he told her, "Barbara, I'm going to be honest with you. I never sent your first resume forward. It was just bad." He'd wisely declined to associate himself with something substandard. Don't put anyone in that awkward position.

The samples that follow give you a "before and after" look at a job candidate's resume. You may look at the "after" version and realize you have a lot of work to do. But resume writing isn't a skill most of us are taught, so don't beat yourself up. From the formatting to the content, it takes time and effort to get it right, but it's always worth it. Even though she'd hired a professional to help her write her resume, Barbara wasn't getting any calls until we did a total rewrite. As her career coach, I gave Barbara lots of homework and we went through four different drafts before she got it right where she needed it to be.

Her original resume lacked the keywords relevant to the project management position she was seeking. (Remember that without those keywords it's highly unlikely recruiters will find your resume.) It also focused too much on describing what her employer had accomplished rather than describing her specific contributions to each project. Barbara posted her new and improved resume and got three calls the second week it was up. Recalibrating her resume was her first step toward securing a job that more than doubled her salary. Don't be surprised if it takes several revisions for you to get your resume in that kind of shape.

BEFORE   AFTER

Visit yvettegavin.com to download a template you can use to design your door-opening resume.

When it has gotten you an interview, your resume has done its work. It opens the door. But once you walk through, it's up to you to speak knowledgably and confidently about the experience and skills you've listed on that document and to demonstrate that you'll be a good fit for the company's culture. It's the interview that will land you or lose you the job.

Quick Recalibration

⊕ Block a time on your calendar this week to do a complete resume revision. Once you make your changes, ask someone whose opinion you trust in this area to give you feedback on your revised resume.

Frequently Asked Resume Questions

Q: How many pages should my resume be?

A: Two to four

Q: Should I use a cover letter?

A: Most of the time it's not needed. However, some recruiters will take a closer look at a resume that has a well-written cover letter.

Q: What do I say in a cover letter?

A: First and foremost, a cover letter needs to be short and concise. I recommend using the information in the Executive Summary of your resume and limiting the letter to three very short paragraphs.

Q: What's the most common cover letter mistake?

A: The biggest error I've seen in cover letters is being addressed to the wrong company. Candidates forget to make the change. The second biggest mistake is misspelled words or incomplete sentences.

Q: What details should I consider when writing the Experience section?

A: When summarizing your experience, speak to the size and scope of your work. Use action verbs to describe your value and accomplishments on a job. (For help with action verbs, go to YvetteGavin.com.)

Use bulleted lists as much as possible. Bullets help you to be concise and make your document easier to read.

Before You Answer the Phone

If you've spent any time in the job market in recent years, you know phone interviews play a big role in today's job search process. The era of having your first interview in the company's human resources office is over for most of us. The higher you climb on the corporate ladder the greater the variety of interview formats and the more likely you'll be screened by a number of different people, from outside recruiters, HR reps, potential peers, and your potential boss, to other managers and executives within the company. Most of the time, it all starts on the phone.

How to Pass the Phone Screen with Flying Colors

1. Answer all calls in a professional manner.
2. Record a businesslike voicemail message for incoming calls.
3. Remain professional.
4. Stand up to make the call.
5. Smile and show your personality.
6. Speak clearly and enunciate.
7. Have your resume on hand and prepare to take notes.
8. Don't get pinned down on salary.
9. Thank the recruiter for calling.

Preparation is key to getting past the initial phone screen and into the room with decision-makers. In a 2014 article published by the Society for Human Resource Management, one HR manager shared that his company disqualifies "approximately 75 percent of candidates based on the initial phone screen."[5] But there's a lot you can do to improve the odds that you won't be one of them.

Once you've posted your well-crafted, attention-grabbing resume on job boards or submitted it directly to the companies you're targeting, you can expect phone calls from recruiters or human resources representatives. (If you're not getting calls you

[5] Tyler, Kathryn. "Be Well-Prepared to Pre-Screen Applicants by Telephone. Http://www.shrm.org/publications/hrmagazine/editorialcontent/2014/0414/pages/0414-telephone-interviews.aspx. April 1, 2014. Accessed December 13, 2015.

need to reassess where you're posting and how your resume reads. It's not too late to recalibrate.) The phone screen serves to verify that you're as good for the position as you appear to be on paper. Too often potential candidates exaggerate their experience, aren't able to articulate their strengths in an interview situation, or lack the necessary social skills to connect with decision-makers. The initial phone conversation weeds out candidates who fall short of the promises made by their resumes.

Since outside recruiters are evaluated and compensated based on how quickly they fill openings, they want to submit a winner. In-house human resources representatives are under just as much pressure to fill a position with the best possible candidate in the shortest possible timeframe. When you receive a recruiting phone call, the person on the other end is hoping to talk to someone who has what it takes to satisfy the hiring manager's requirements. If they feel good about your performance on this phone call and your responses indicate you're a solid match, they'll move you on to the next phase.

When you're actively searching for a new job and expecting recruiters to call, you should always answer the phone in a professional manner, just as you would in the office. Be especially vigilant if the call is from an unknown number or a number you don't recognize.

———— • ————

Remember:
Your resume opens the
door for a conversation.
The interview lands the job.

———— • ————

When you take an incoming call, simply state your first and last names as you would in the office. "This is Yvette Gavin." But use your own name!

With everything you have going on it's easy to get caught off guard and answer a call too casually or even inappropriately when you're not prepared for it. While a professional phone demeanor is a must, I recommend you go a step farther and let every call that comes from a number you don't recognize go to voicemail. Of course, your voicemail message should sound businesslike. No slow jams or music of any kind. No kids singing cute songs. No barking dog or romantic messages with your sweetheart. A simple confirmation of who the caller has reached is best.

When you get a voicemail notification, check it right away. Then take a moment to compose yourself. Make sure you have a positive attitude. If you're feeling stressed, rushed, or distracted, this is your chance to recalibrate your mental state and bring out your best self so you can make the right impression. Your mindset will come through clearly over the phone, and it matters.

Before you punch up that number, make sure you're in an environment you can control. You do not want to ask a recruiter to hold for a minute while you yell at your children to stop slamming doors or wait for the lawnmower outside your window to stop running. Grab your resume and a pad and pen to jot down notes or get the recruiter's contact information. Now you're ready to return that call.

Making the Call

Recruiters typically have a lot of candidates to contact, so return the call as soon as you can. Call the recruiter from a quiet space with your most professional, engaging persona on display. Forget about sitting at the kitchen table. Stand while you're making the call. You'll have more energy and confidence than when you're seated, and that comes across in your voice. This is especially important for women because standing helps your voice project with more strength. Remember the person on the other end of the call can't judge you on body language, attire, or appearance. Beyond the quality of your answers, your personality and voice are your only ways to distinguish yourself.

It's helpful if you can stand in front of a mirror to keep an eye on your expressions. I usually do phone interviews in front of my bathroom mirror. I have my resume and notepad on the counter and glance at my reflection periodically to make sure I'm projecting a friendly demeanor. It's easy to take on a serious tone when you're talking about work, but you want to maintain good posture and smile throughout the phone interview. The warmth you display will come through in your voice and make it easier for the recruiter to connect with you.

Do your best to neutralize any accent or speech quirk you may have. I'm from a small town in the South, and I have to moderate my accent when I'm in a professional setting, especially in the interview process. People do have biases against certain regions, ethnicities, and other differences that your voice or speech pattern may reflect. For instance, I'm aware that people with Southern accents are sometimes stereotyped as ignorant or racist, so I don't want the recruiter to get Georgia as soon as I open my mouth. I'd prefer that recruiters hear how my experience is a perfect match for the position before making other judgments about me. Of course, this is less important if the job is in a Southern state, but I still use my most neutral, professional voice.

On the other hand, I'm fairly sure that anyone who talks to me on the phone will identify me as African American. That's not something I try to hide. Instead, I make sure I sound like an African American professional. I've seen talented people struggle to advance because they used slang or some local dialect in the workplace. In a previous job, for example, I worked with a contractor who applied over and over for a full-time position within the company she was contracted to work with. They rejected her every time. Her performance was good enough to keep her on as a contractor, but her English had such a street edge they wouldn't seriously consider her as someone who'd represent the company as a full-time employee.

This wasn't a case of racism in the workplace. They didn't decline to bring her on as a full-time employee because she was African American. They turned her down because she talked like she was hanging out with her friends, not working in a professional environment. Leave the slang at home. Practice as much as you need to, but learn to speak like the corporate success story you plan to become.

If English is your second language and you have a heavy accent that native English-speakers sometimes struggle to understand, consider getting some accent modification training. This isn't about erasing your culture. This is about giving yourself the best possible chance to land your dream job and earn the salary you desire. I'm telling you this as someone who has been in the hiring manager's seat and had to turn down candidates for just this reason.

In one instance, I conducted a phone interview with a woman named Charlotte. When she came on the line I was surprised to hear a heavy East Asian accent. Although she had the right qualifications on paper I couldn't offer her the job because I couldn't understand much of what she said. I couldn't ask my team to work alongside someone who couldn't effectively collaborate with them because of an accent barrier.

No matter what your first language or where you're from, speak clearly. Enunciate your words, and if there are certain words you struggle with pronouncing, think of some synonyms and use them instead. The quality of your speech should reflect how bright, experienced, and right for the job you are and leave a recruiter impressed with your professionalism.

Finally, if you reach voicemail when you return the recruiter's call, leave a clear and concise message including your name, phone number, and reference to the fact that you're responding to a message you received from him or her.

Questions to Expect on a Phone Interview

In these initial conversations with recruiters and HR reps, expect general questions to confirm the information on your resume. They'll also want to get a fix on your personality and an idea of whether or not you'd be a fit for the company culture. A recruiter isn't likely to have specific knowledge about the job you're applying for, but she may ask a few position-specific questions suggested by the hiring manager. Every recruiter wants to find the superstar candidate, the person who can land the job, so give them every reason to believe you're the one. Answer the questions to the best of your ability, and let your personality shine through.

What kind of salary are you looking for?

If you've done your research, you know how much the job you're interested in typically pays, but that doesn't mean you should answer this question. Recruiters will try to nail you down on a salary expectation. But if your answer is too low you'll lock yourself in at the bottom of the pay scale. If it's too high, they'll put your resume aside even though the company might be willing to raise the salary range for the right candidate.

Instead of answering with a number, tell the recruiter you'd like to learn more about the role and that you'd like to have a conversation about the specific responsibilities before you talk about salary. However, this may be a good time to make it clear you're not looking to make a lateral move. There's no need to waste time if the potential salary is well below what you find acceptable or the job is a wrong fit.

If the recruiter insists on getting a salary figure, provide a salary range, but never, never, never lock yourself in at one number.

What do you make in your current position?

Again, do not let the recruiter force you into giving a specific number. You might say, "I earn market value for my current position as a _____." You can also give a range, but when you do, make sure you factor in all the benefits that come with your job. This might include vacation time, educational benefits, bonuses, or other extras. For instance, when I worked for a major airline one of the benefits was free air travel for my family and me. When I left the airline I had to give that up, so I factored that into the numbers I shared as my current salary range.

What are you looking for in a new position?

This question opens the door for you to share your values and demonstrate how you might fit into the company's culture. It's also meant to see if your goals align with what the position offers and what the hiring manager wants. Reference your skills and how you want to use and continue to develop them as well as your long-term goals and the things that motivate you in a job.

Here's an example of a solid answer to the question:

"I'm looking for an opportunity to leverage my leadership skills in growing and developing highly proficient QA teams while expanding my knowledge of the telecommunications industry."

This answer covers a current strength and shows off the candidate's value-add while also expressing a potential growth opportunity the position could offer the candidate.

Questions to Ask on a Phone Interview

Asking questions demonstrates that you're engaged and interested. It also shows you're not willing to take whatever job you happen to come across. A recruiter doesn't know the position the way the hiring manager will, but you can still ask some basic questions. Depending on who the call is with and what you already know, consider asking:

- How long has the position been open?
- What's the reason the position is open?
- Where is the position located?
- What is the job description for this position?
- What are the next steps in the process?

If you really can't think of a question in the moment, simply say, "I did have a couple of questions, but you've already answered them." You'll compliment the recruiter for doing her job so thoroughly, which is certainly better than saying, "No, I don't have anything to ask."

As the recruiter wraps up the call, make sure you thank him for contacting you and let him know you look forward to learning more about this position. That last impression counts just as much as the first.

When You're Not Really Looking for a Job

Once your resume is posted on job boards you may get calls even when you're not actively looking. If a recruiter asks if you're still in the job market, hear him out. Even when I'm very happy in my position and not in an active job search, I don't shy away from recruiters' calls.

When asked if I'm still interested in a career move, I say, "I'm always open for a conversation." That's because I've learned opportunities can appear when you're not looking for them. I landed a dream position in telecommunications because I took the time to talk with a recruiter even though I wasn't focused on changing jobs at that time. Because I remained open, my career took a whole new trajectory.

Take these phone screens just as seriously as you would face-to-face interviews and handle them with preparedness and professionalism. The recruiter had a stack of resumes to go through and chose to call you. You made the first cut, and this phone call is your chance to win an ally who can push you through to the next phase. You want the recruiter to hang up the phone ready to recommend you and sell you to the hiring manager as her favorite candidate.

Quick Recalibration

⊕ Print a few copies of your resume and stash them in places where you can easily access them when you have a phone interview. Don't forget your bathroom cabinet!

⊕ How do you sound on the phone? Ask someone you know and trust to give you specific feedback on your phone voice and demeanor. Make any necessary improvements and regularly practice those changes. If you don't have a trusted friend for this exercise, consider recording your own voice so you can critically listen to yourself.

One on One, Face to Face

Once you make it past the phone screening, your next step will usually be a face-to-face interview at one of the company's locations. It's critical that you think about and prepare for every aspect of this part of the process before you walk in to meet the hiring manager or panel of interviewers. Thorough planning will help you put your best self forward and ease the nervousness you're likely to feel going into an interview. Your preparation starts with taking on the right mindset.

Your Interview Mindset

The thought of being judged on and quizzed about your professional knowledge and work experience is enough to make anyone nervous. Fortunately, there's a lot you can do to recalibrate your mindset and be ready to handle the interview like a pro.

The onsite, one-on-one interview is what most people think about when they think of the interview process, and it's a make-or-break part of the job search. There are several steps to preparing for this face-to-face conversation, but when you take them one at a time, they're all manageable. When the day arrives you'll look, talk, and act like the best candidate for the job.

How you think about yourself and about the hiring process will affect everything you do. It all starts with knowing you have options. If you've taken the time to discover your unique value using the exercises shared earlier in this book, you know what you bring to the table. You know this isn't just a matter of whether the interviewer is interested in you. You're also going into the interview process to assess whether the company would be a good fit for you and your career goals. No matter how much research you've done you need more information to decide if you want this job. Look at the interview as a conversation. Both sides are trying to get to know one another and assess whether they should move forward with a working relationship.

It's also important to remember your why. What will this job change mean for your career, for your personal happiness, and for your family's well-being? Why is landing your dream job at the salary you desire so important to you? How will your daily life improve once you're earning the salary you desire?

Interview Story-Shaping Exercise

This is an important exercise that can help you become the person you want to be in your professional life. Take some time to visualize how you want the interviewer to perceive you. Make notes for yourself about what you want to say to your interviewer so you can shape a story in her mind based on the image of yourself you want to project. Use these notes to select the right terms, phrases, and stories when you practice your interview answers.

Role Model Image Exercise

When Barbara came to me for coaching she had a goal of earning a salary in the high six-figures. At that point, however, she didn't yet present herself as someone who made that kind of money. I walked her through another exercise to help her begin to present herself in a more polished and professional way. The same exercise that helped Barbara can help you.

First, think of a person who already has the position you want or who makes the salary you're trying to reach. This person is your role model for this exercise. List the positive characteristics he or she has, from appearance and attire to professional skills, demeanor, and way of speaking. Be as specific as you can.

Now go back and rate yourself on a scale of 1 to 10 on each of those attributes. It's okay if you're nowhere near where you want to be in some or even most areas. If you're a 5 in your industry vocabulary, for example, decide what you can do to reach a 7. Trying to leap to a 10 right away can be difficult and scary, but you can get there over time. With incremental progress, you'll eventually find you can comfortably achieve the standard you've set for yourself based on your role model.

After I went through this exercise with Barbara, she shared with me that I was the person she'd visualized. I certainly took that as a compliment. But the point was that no matter who it was, she could get to where her role model was. So can you.

Doing the Right Research

Of course, you've already done your research on the company, or you wouldn't have agreed to interview for a position there. If for some reason you haven't, don't make the mistake of going into an interview without understanding some of the following basics:

- What products or services does the company offer?
- What clients do they serve?
- Is the company privately held or publicly traded?
- Who are their primary competitors?
- What are the current major company initiatives?
- What makes you a good fit for the company?

In one interview with a firm that had just gone public, I congratulated my interviewer on an award the company had won a few months earlier. He responded, "Wow! We won that?" Instead of just sitting there answering questions, I was able to bring in information I'd discovered through my research to demonstrate that I was a person who kept abreast of the latest industry news. Undoubtedly, it distinguished me from the other candidates, and yes, I got that job.

No matter what role you're applying for you should have some real knowledge of the company, but the level of the position will dictate the kind of information you'll be expected to know. For example, a candidate for an executive position should have much more high-level knowledge than an individual contributor, so take that into consideration.

As you prep for your interview, take some time to review your research so you can speak intelligently about the company and be prepared to ask questions that demonstrate you've done your homework. You should also look closely at the details of the job description. That way you can address any specific skillset or experience they want.

However, your research doesn't stop there. If the human resources representative doesn't tell you exactly who you'll be interviewing with, ask for the names and titles of everyone you can expect to meet in your interview. This is critical. It allows you to do an Internet search on each individual who'll be involved in the decision of whether or not you'll be getting a job offer. Check out their LinkedIn profiles and posts too. This isn't cyber-stalking. This is good

Review your resume before an interview

sense. Understanding an interviewer's position, work history, and education will help you predict what kinds of questions he or she is likely to ask, since people tend to bend their questions toward their own areas of expertise. If you know who you'll be interacting with, you can better anticipate the theme of their questions.

Run another search to find out what kinds of questions companies like the one you're interviewing with typically ask. There's a surprising amount of information available about the specific interview processes used by larger companies. In one case, I found some of the exact interview questions a large telecomm company asked candidates. I went into the interview expecting to be asked one specific question and with full knowledge of what I should say even though the question wasn't directly relevant to the job. Sure enough, they asked, and I answered. I did get the job, but I later recommended they stop asking that irrelevant question.

Interview Practice

If interviews typically make you nervous or you have limited interview experience, you should definitely do a mock interview. Based on your research, pull together a list of questions you expect to be asked and have a friend sit down and interview you from that list.

I've been through a lot of interviews, on both sides of the table, so I no longer do a mock interview every time, but I always rehearse my answers for the questions I anticipate. It doesn't really matter whether I have the exact questions the interviewer will ask. This rehearsal helps me get back into interview mode. I practice playing up my strengths and correcting my weaknesses. For instance, I learned early in my career that I have a tendency to talk, and talk, and talk, in response to a question. I have to make sure I'm prepared to answer a direct question in a direct way so I don't ramble. Rehearsal helps me do that.

Whether you rehearse in front of a mirror or have someone put you through a complete mock interview, pay attention to your body language and your voice. You want to sound warm and confident. Smile and make eye contact with the interviewer. Practice will help you hone your thought processes, your vocabulary, your body language, and your attitude.

Questions to Expect in the Interview

To start with, see yourself on the other side of the desk and think about what you would want to know about the person who may fill this position. You can expect most interviewers to ask open-ended questions, questions you can't answer with a simple yes or no. In addition, most companies employ situational questions. These typically start with something like, "How would you handle_____?" They're meant to get you to reveal how you would apply the skills you list on your resume in real world situations.

Interviewers will often lead you to tell a story. They might say something like, "Tell me about a time when you had to____." These types of questions are designed to show how you've handled specific situations, but they'll also reveal your attitude about a variety of things. People tend to let more of themselves slip out when they're telling a story, so be aware of the slant you put on your answer.

Regardless of the industry you're in or the position you're applying for, there are some things you're likely to be asked at some point in your job search. Sometimes those that seem the simplest can trip you up the most. Let's look at a few of these.

Tell me about yourself?

I'm amazed at some of the things that come out of a candidate's mouth in response to this inquiry. Hiring managers don't want to hear that you're the youngest of fourteen kids or that you've recently gotten a divorce. They want to get a feel for your personality and understand what skills and experiences make you the best fit for the job. They want to know about your professional self and what kind of person they'll be working with if you join the team.

Tell me about your current position?

For some reason, many people answer this by thinking about the job description and sharing which parts of it they can't do or haven't yet done. Stay away from negatives. Your response should focus on your job responsibilities and what you've accomplished. This isn't the time to recount all the great things your company has done either. You need to describe how you've contributed to the company's achievements. Remember that you're selling you, not the company you're leaving.

What's your greatest weakness?

You do not want to give anybody anything they can use to disqualify you for this position. If your answer is that you tend to be late to work, you sometimes miss deadlines, or you have trouble getting along with people, you can kiss that job goodbye.

I once interviewed a gentleman for a job that required a good deal of writing. When asked about his greatest weakness he explained that he didn't have a good grasp of English grammar and vocabulary. I'm sure this was an honest answer, but it immediately took him out of the running for the position.

Your answer should be a positive aspect of your character shaped as a weakness. For example, most people want to work with team players. I might say my weakness is that I've often found myself working late to help a struggling colleague after I've completed my own projects, and it throws off my work-life balance. That answer demonstrates that I care about my co-workers and know how to be a contributing part of a team. It's an honest answer that focuses on one of my strengths, and any company that wouldn't appreciate that about me probably isn't somewhere I want to work.

If you could have any superpower, which would you choose and why?

This is the type of offbeat question some companies are asking candidates these days. They're designed to test your composure or creativity, to reveal your problem-solving skills or character, or to determine how well you think on your feet. If you come across some of these in your research of the company's standard interview questions, go ahead and prepare for them.

Whatever the unconventional question actually is, it's important not to panic when you hear it. Most of the time there's no right answer. As long as your response is articulate and based in some logic, you should be okay. If it makes you less nervous you can always do an Internet search for "weird interview questions" and practice your answers in advance. There are even websites that will throw you one curveball question after another. When in doubt, give one of those a try.

How many children do you have?

This is an example of a question that should never be asked in an interview. Most interviewers are aware that they shouldn't inquire about marital status, gender, sexual preference, whether or not you have children, or any specific details about your family and personal life. In a professional environment, this shouldn't be a problem. However, if you run into a question like this, keep your composure and steer the conversation back to one of your strengths or remarkable accomplishments. If the interviewer continues to press you on it there's a good chance that isn't a place you want to work.

Dress for the Job—and the Money—You Want

Recently a co-worker approached me to share the fact that her mentor had advised her to model her attire after mine to increase her chances of moving up in the company. Of course it's always nice to be seen in such a light, but she also explained that what she really wanted to talk about was my choice of red lipstick for work. (But that's a topic for the next section.)

I wasn't always the sharpest dresser in the office. When I decided to manage my own career I looked around and identified the professionals who presented themselves with the kind of image I wanted to project. I landed on the always-polished consultants who worked in our office. These were men who typically showed up in starched, button-down, white shirts and dark blue suits. I wanted to be where they were, so that was the look I decided to emulate, particularly for interviews. It's a classic style, clean and professional, and it has never failed me in a business setting.

If you look in my closet, you'll find an extraordinary number of crisp white shirts. That's because I buy a new one for every interview. Yes, every single one. White shirts can quickly start to get dingy over a short period of time, and I want to look as polished as I can. Dingy just won't do it.

I love my white shirt and blue suit ensemble, but there's a caveat. While you have to decide what looks right for you based on your personal taste, goals, and target job, I typically steer my female clients away from wearing a pant suit on an initial interview. You just don't know what kind of bias the person sitting across from you might have. It might seem archaic, but it's not worth the risk. Besides a skirt suit, a nice dress paired with a blazer is also a good choice. Save the pants for later.

Dress professionally for an interview, even if the work environment dress code is casual.

On several occasions I've gotten confirmation that dressing the part really does pay off. After I was hired for a particular telecommunications position, I asked my boss why he chose me out of all the candidates they considered. "Yvette," he told me, "you looked like money when you walked in that door."

When you "look like money," you send a message that you're not desperate for a job and you won't be had for any old mediocre offer they put on the table. You send a message that you have other options.

You can bend some of the rules on interview appearance when you're looking for work in an artistic or alternative industry or a company that has a very casual culture. But be careful. Just because the employees dress down doesn't mean you should for the interview. It can be rather presumptuous to show up for an interview dressed as if you already work there. Even if the company dress code is relaxed, your interview attire should be a step above the norm to demonstrate the seriousness you're bringing to the interview process.

While you should never depend on your looks to get you a job, you can't afford to underestimate the importance of appearance in this process. Years ago a friend and I both applied for a job at a cable news network, and it came down to the two of us. She was a graduate of a prestigious college, and I hadn't finished my degree.

She was a sophisticated woman who grew up in a big city, and I was a small town girl who'd experienced much less of the world. However, she had a tendency to wear her hair pulled back in a ponytail with a scarf tied around her forehead while I always maintained a professional look. In the end, I was the one who got the job.

As is my habit, I later asked my boss why he chose me, and I'll never forget his answer. "Yvette, when you have two equally qualified candidates, and you're confident that both can do the job but one is more pleasing to the eye than the other, that's the one you go with. I have to look at you every day." Is that fair? Maybe not. But I don't make the rules. I just make the most of them.

Hair Matters

My friend lost that position to me partly because she didn't make an effort to look her best. The appropriateness of certain hairstyles can be a sensitive subject, especially among women, and even more so for African American women, but it's an aspect of interview preparedness you can't afford to overlook. In fact, it's something you need to be aware of and make fully informed decisions about as you create your professional image on the job or in your job search every day. I learned this lesson early in my career when I worked for a major newspaper.

There was a young woman on the staff who'd always impressed me. She had a great education from a top university. She was a strong writer, and she generously took the time to coach me and give me feedback on my work so I could turn in stronger pieces. One day she came in to work with a new look. Overnight, she'd gone from straightened hair to a short afro. You'd better believe that new hairdo became the news in the newsroom.

I was shocked to hear all the buzz about a simple haircut, but I was even more shocked when, a week later, I found her cleaning out her desk. Even though she was one of our strongest writers, she'd been relegated to one of the satellite offices, a place where the paper usually sent younger, unseasoned reporters so they could get some experience on the community newspapers and work their way up. She cried as she packed her things, and when I asked her what happened, she told me she was sure it was all about her hair.

That scenario happened in the 1980s, but don't fool yourself into thinking it can't happen today. I've met with my fellow panel members to debrief after interviewing a candidate and had whole conversations about a woman's hair. In one case, they refused to promote an internal candidate because of her long "Bo Derek" braids.

I protested that she was qualified for the position, but they wouldn't budge. The new job would require her to meet with internal customers, and the interview panel members thought she lacked the necessary professional image.

I never shared with her the real reason she didn't get that promotion, but I did give her some coaching before her next internal interview. This time she showed up with the braids taken down, her hair straightened, and a weave put in. She wore my favorite interview outfit: a blue suit with a white shirt. One of the panel members commented that he didn't even recognize her. Since she would be on my team, I made the hiring decision, but I didn't face any opposition when I chose to offer her the position.

I'm not standing on a soapbox to tell anyone you can't wear braids, dreadlocks, twists, or any other unconventional hairstyle. In fact, my son wears his hair in twists. For him it's a spiritual expression, so no amount of career coaching is going to make him change it. Instead, he created an opportunity to address his personal style in his job interview, and he was able to land a great job after college and quickly advanced within the company.

The truth is, though, we still live in a world where people, especially women, are judged on appearance. Any hairstyle you choose should always look neat and well-groomed. But in conventional, conservative corporate cultures, some of the natural styles we love can lock you out of a job. As more African Americans take positions of leadership this might become less problematic, but regardless of a person's race, you can never be sure how you'll be judged based on anything considered outside the norm.

I coach my clients to wear their hair in a more conservative style for the interview process. You should make your best effort to have your hair professionally done. I'll tell you that I would live on peanut butter for a week if I needed to scrape up the cash to get my hair done for an interview. But if you don't, at least pull your hair back in a neat, polished bun. I know the value of creating a professional image. I've experienced it firsthand.

If you love your hairstyle and don't think it will negatively affect the way people at work respond to you, you can return to it after you get the job. If it's a part of you that you don't wish to change at all, so be it. You're well within your rights to make that choice, but consider that it may affect your job prospects, and you need to do everything you can to offset that possibility.

Makeup and Accessories

Earlier I mentioned the woman who told me she was modeling her business attire after mine who questioned my choice of red lipstick. She'd recently purchased a shade of red for herself, but she assumed it was too sexy to wear at work. The shade I wore that day was a soft, matte red that complimented my outfit. It was perfectly appropriate for the office, as I explained to her, but I wouldn't choose it for an interview.

In an interview situation you're still trying to get the job. You never know when a decision-maker will be offended by something you think of as perfectly fine or even stylish. In this modern age there are still people who see red lipstick as too provocative for work, regardless of how muted it is. For interviews, keep your makeup and accessories clean, polished, and neutral. And get a professional manicure.

Good news for women: we've moved beyond a need to wear stockings, so unless that's your personal preference, you don't need them. If you choose to wear peep-toe shoes, a pedicure is an absolute necessity. Closed-toe heels that are a comfortable height for you, but not so high as to seem unprofessional, are the safest choice for an interview, especially your first with a new company.

If you don't believe a pair of shoes can make a real difference, consider a client I worked with who wanted to move to Manhattan. When a company flew her to the city for an interview, she was excited and did her best to prepare. Thinking she might have an opportunity to do some sightseeing, she arrived to the interview wearing flats. Unfortunately, someone greeted her in the lobby as soon as she stepped through the door and immediately swept her away to her meeting with a director and a vice-president. She never had a chance to switch to the heels she had in her bag, so what would've been a polished image ended up looking unfinished and unsophisticated. New York City certainly isn't the place to look unfashionable. She didn't get the job, and when she asked the recruiter for feedback, the list of things she could've done better included her shoes.

What to Carry into the Interview

Along with shoes, many of us ladies love our purses. Maybe you have a collection of high-end designer bags, neatly organized by size and color, lining the shelves of your closet. I hate to tell you this, but none of them should make it into the interview with you. While men may not notice, unfortunately, some women will hone in on your purse as a way to make quick, superficial assessments of your character. If your purse appears cheap by their standards, they'll lower their opinion of you. If it's a designer brand they can't afford or makes them wonder how you can afford it, they may hold it against you or decide it must be a knock-off and draw negative conclusions about you.

Lock your purse in the trunk of your car and carry a nice portfolio with a notepad and pen inside. On the second page of the notepad make a list of a few questions you want to ask during the interview. These inquiries should come out naturally if you've prepared, but if you draw a blank, you can casually refer to your list. Don't write them on the first page of the pad. You don't want anyone peeking over your shoulder to see what you've written.

Separate your car key and fob from your other keys and tuck them into one of the interior pockets of the portfolio. The one I carry has a business card holder where my key fits perfectly. You should also include extra copies of your resume, and if it's relevant to your position, you can bring along samples of your work.

Interview Wardrobe Don'ts

A purse isn't the only thing you should leave out of your interview attire. Other basic wardrobe don'ts include:

- Visible tattoos
- Visible body or facial piercings
- Excessive cleavage
- Gaudy or excessive jewelry
- Tight clothing
- Short skirts
- Overdone makeup or perfume

That list may seem overly conservative for this day and age, but remember many corporate cultures are still very traditional, especially older, privately-held companies. I've seen a manager reject a job candidate simply because the woman had a small tattoo on her ankle. Because the manager thought of tattoos as unprofessional, the candidate's qualifications were completely discounted.

If you have tattoos or other forms of body art, it's in your best interest to cover them for an interview and perhaps even after you get the job. There's a good chance lots of your co-workers will be doing the same thing.

In one post-interview debrief, my male colleagues spent all their time debating whether a man's earring was in the ear that meant he was straight or the one that meant he was gay—and this wasn't very long ago. Imagine how those same hiring managers would react to a woman with a nose ring or six piercings in each ear. These things that seem like a part of you, because you've grown accustomed to them, can be off-putting to some of the people who have the power to give you the job and the salary you desire. Take out or cover your piercings.

Ultimately, women have more to think about when it comes to attire, and it's always risky for a woman to wear anything that can be construed as provocative. Women are regularly denied promotions and turned down for jobs because their choice of clothing made someone uncomfortable. I've worked in male-dominated industries, and several men, including some executives, have made it clear they don't want to work next to a woman who wears tight clothing or shows what they consider to be too much cleavage. They're certainly not going to hire anyone who they'll have to avoid at work every day.

Ladies, it's not fair, but you can either fight for your right to wear what you like or you can choose to be more conservative in your dress and land the position you really want, the kind of job that helps you fulfill the why behind your career moves.

The Day of the Interview

You've selected your interview outfit, copies of your resume are in your portfolio, and you've got a mock interview or two under your belt. Even after you've done everything you can to prepare, it's normal to get the jitters before an interview. I still get nervous at times too, but it's important to go into it with a peaceful state of mind. One of the ways I achieve that sense of calm is to rely on my faith.

Before an interview, I ask God to open the hearts and minds of the persons I will meet. I ask that I might have the right words to communicate my knowledge, experience, and ideas in a way that the interviewer can receive them. I've sat on panels in which the person on my left interpreted a candidate's words completely differently from the person on my right. Things can easily get misconstrued through an individual's personal filters, so I pray that God grants me the ability to be in tune with each individual and adjust my terminology and demeanor to communicate with him or her as effectively as possible.

When I coach people of faith, I do advise them to use prayer to prepare for an interview, and they've consistently said it helps them to be their best selves in what can be a stressful situation. However, you don't have to be a religious person to center yourself and adopt the best possible state of mind before an interview. You can meditate or simply find a place to sit in silence and quiet your mind.

Another way to take some of the stress out of the interview process is to plan to arrive at the location thirty minutes early. That way you don't have to worry about potential traffic snarls making you late. In fact, I'll often drive to the interview location the day before my scheduled interview to make sure I won't have any trouble finding it. If you live in a city with unpredictable traffic delays, you should give yourself even more leeway. There's rarely a good excuse to be late to an interview.

Once you arrive at the site, your interview has already begun. You never know who will see you in the parking lot or the lobby of the building. Greet every person you meet in a friendly, professional manner. That's just common decency, but you should also remember the receptionist you're short with or the security guard you're rude to might just have the hiring manager's ear. You'd be shocked at the influence someone in a position some people would consider "unimportant" can actually have with decision-makers. Don't risk blowing your opportunity before you get to the official interview.

If you arrive early, you don't have to go in right away. No one wants to see you an hour before your appointment. Use the extra time to go over your resume one last time and refresh your memory with the language on it. It's not necessarily the vocabulary you use every day, so this quick review will help you pull in industry terms during the interview, and it will also increase your level of confidence.

Once you've done that, you can go in ten or fifteen minutes early. In that case, always let the receptionist or whoever greets you know you're there, but be sure to mention that you're early. This small note is critical. You never want to create a bad first impression by making the hiring manager feel pressured because you arrived too early and he or she isn't ready for you.

This is a good time to take a moment to go to the restroom and give yourself a once-over in the mirror. Make sure you look as polished and put together as you did when you left home.

What to Do in the Interview

When you're being introduced to someone or introducing yourself, always extend your hand for a greeting. This is particularly important for women because many traditional men have a belief that they should wait for a woman to initiate a handshake. If you don't do it, neither will they. Do the same at the end of the interview as you thank each person for his or her time and for considering you for the position.

Recently, I attended a conference that included college students. One student shook my hand and his palm was actually wet. I wanted to run to the restroom and wash. It just wasn't a good feeling to have someone's damp hand clasped in mine. If you know you have a problem with sweaty palms, carry a tissue or handkerchief in your pocket and discretely dry your hand before extending it to someone.

You don't want to come into a new space and drop into a chair as if you're overly familiar with your interviewer. Wait until you're invited to be seated. If that doesn't happen, you can ask a question such as, "Where would you like me to sit?"

Just as in the phone interview, you want to come across as warm, friendly, accessible, and confident. Smile and make eye contact. If you're in the interviewer's office, glance around the room. Is there something with which you can make a personal connection? Maybe there's a picture of a child playing soccer. If your child just won a college scholarship for soccer, you might find a time to bring it up in the interview. If there's a club membership plaque on the wall, and you're also a member of that club, it might bear mentioning.

The interview is a time for you to assess if the role is a good fit for you

You're scanning for something that will connect the two of you on a personal level and make you memorable among the pool of candidates. But don't force it. If you're in a generic conference room or the office has few personal details, don't worry. That kind of small talk isn't a necessity for a strong interview performance, but your positive and engaging personality is highly important. I can't count the number of times quality candidates were removed from consideration because they "lacked personality."

At the end of the day, people want to work with folks they like, connect with, and feel comfortable being around. The days of hiring staff solely based on skills are long gone. Personality matters, so you should always go into an interview prepared to express your best professional self. Be engaging, warm, and friendly. Recently, a C-suite executive shared with me that she's encouraging her staff to hire personality first and skills second. "Skills can be taught and learned," she said, "but personality, not so much."

Any time you want to connect with people, eye contact is highly important. Don't overlook this point. If you're being interviewed by a panel, be sure to give each person at the table eye contact at least once as you speak. During panel interviews, you want to engage everyone. Giving eye contact to each interviewer when answering or asking a question shows you're having a conversation with each of them, not just the one or two interviewers with whom you feel most comfortable.

During the interview, jot down a few important notes in your notepad, but continue to make eye contact. Don't spend all your time bent over your portfolio writing every word as you did in ninth-grade biology class. You want to demonstrate that you're interested, not come across as uncomfortable or distracted.

To this day, I vividly remember the male candidate who, in a panel interview, looked at me and ignored everyone else. My boss was part of this interview panel, and she didn't take it kindly when the candidate focused on me while answering her questions. Throughout our interaction, he barely turned his head to look at my boss, who had the authority and power to make the final decision on who got the position. I felt so badly for the candidate. I wanted to tell him to stop looking at me and focus a little more on all the people at the table, but of course, that didn't happen. Do I really need to tell you after that interview my boss had no interest in discussing that candidate's fitness for the job?

Don't forget the interview is also a time for you to assess whether or not this company is a good fit for you. Be prepared to ask your own questions. Some will arise naturally, but as mentioned earlier, you should have a few written on the second page of your notepad. You certainly want to know who you would report to, for instance, so if that information isn't shared, be sure to ask. Pay attention to the physical environment and the way people treat each other and you. These details will play an important part in whether you actually want to accept the position when it's offered.

No matter how much you've prepared, some inquiries by the interviewer may still catch you off guard. If you need a minute to gather your thoughts, start by rephrasing the question, as if you're trying to make sure you understand it correctly. Sometimes, but not always, the interviewer will repeat the question in a slightly different way. This will buy you a little time to order your thoughts.

As a hiring manager, I've seen candidates shut down by irrelevant questions. In a panel interview, one of my colleagues asked a candidate to rank, on a scale of 1 to 10, her mastery of a specific skillset that was not a job requirement. When she ranked herself fairly highly, my colleague went on to ask her a very technical question, which she couldn't answer. He shot her down and told her she actually couldn't even rate herself as a 1 in that area. His unnecessary criticism completely deflated her. The problem I had with the whole interaction was that she'd been trapped by a line of questioning that told us nothing about her ability to do the job. Unfortunately, she didn't know how to redirect the conversation.

If the question is about a skill that seems to have little or nothing to do with the prospective position, remember that people ask questions about areas in which they are most comfortable. Turn it back on the interviewer by explaining that you understood the job required X. Ask if they're now saying it requires Y. This will usually get things back on track.

When the interview is wrapping up, the hiring manager or whoever has led the conversation should advise you as to the next steps in the process and how soon you can expect to hear something. If not, make sure you ask. You don't want to sit around waiting for days or weeks because you have no idea what their process might be. As you leave, remember that your interview isn't over until you pull out of the parking lot, drive away from the office, and get home. No ignoring "the little people" because you're in a rush or flying into road rage as you try to make it out of a packed parking lot. Remain professional, polite, and kind.

When Applying to an Internal Job

When interviewing for a job within the company with which you're currently employed, don't treat it lightly. You have to do the same due diligence as if you were applying to a new company. If the position is not in your current department, research the group and its goals. Don't dress for the interview as if it's just another day in your regular job. Show up with the same polished look you'd be expected to have if you were an external candidate. While it helps that you've already made connections within your company, you may also have to combat any negative image people have of you. It doesn't matter if you deserve that image or not. If it exists, it's up to you to correct it by taking control of your image.

If you're applying for a management position for the first time, you have to help your co-workers see you as a manager by presenting that image. If you're making the jump to the executive level, let them see you dress, talk, and work like an executive. Apply the steps in this book to polish your resume, prepare for your interview, and do everything you possibly can to improve your chances of landing the job you want with the salary you desire right where you are.

Quick Recalibration

⊕ Complete the Story-shaping and Image Role Model exercises. Choose one characteristic from the second exercise and make a small recalibration to improve your score in that area today.

⊕ Choose your role model for the position you want. With that image in mind, make a list of the items you need to style your perfect interview image. Plan to shop for them as soon as it fits your budget. If money is tight, go to www.YvetteGavin.com/professionalattire for a list of professional clothing stores where you can shop on a smaller budget.

⊕ Do an Internet search for "common interview questions for_____," filling in the blank with an industry you want to work in or job you want to apply for. Compile a list of questions and use them for your interview practice.

Yvette,

Thank you so much for all of your coaching tonight. You provided incredible insight and mentoring. I am going to go through all your recommendations and update my document for future reference.
In addition, I will send a friendly reminder to the CIO on Friday. I really feel CONFIDENT now after your Coaching Tonight!

I look forward to reading your book, Recalibrate! Navigating the Job Market with Confidence."

You are AWESOME!!!

Barbara

After the Interview

You've gotten through the hard part, but the position isn't yours yet, so don't let up on your focus. How you behave after the interview can push you over the top or cost you the job.

Say Thank You

It took me a long time to accept the fact that the days of sending a handwritten thank you note after an interview are pretty much over. I really like that personal touch, but I'm afraid your personalized stationary and a good pen are no longer your best options. When you mail a letter, it can take days or weeks to make it through the post office and the mailroom to the person you're trying to reach. It's still important to send a thank you note, but email is a much more efficient and reliable option.

While some people like to email a thank you immediately, I prefer to wait a day or two. Following your interview, you're already at the top of their minds, so you may benefit more by bringing yourself back to their attention days later, during which time they've likely seen other candidates and memory of your sterling performance may have started to fade. You can write it the same day, while the interview is still fresh in your mind, but hold off sending it right away.

Keep your email simple and to the point. It's always great if you can mention something you discussed, so refer to your notes. If you interviewed with more than one person, send them each the same email. You don't want them to start comparing how you responded to one person differently than to another. It does happen, and it's an unnecessary distraction that could work against you.

Before you hit send, make sure you've addressed the right person and company. Check, double-check, and triple-check your spelling and grammar. An error here could be fatal to your chances of getting the job, so have a friend who writes well review it if you don't feel confident in your own writing skills.

The Right References

Your potential employers will ask for references when they're ready for them, so you should always have your list of three solid contacts ready. Whoever you choose, make sure that person is aware you want to use them as a reference. I've actually had to decline to serve for someone who asked me to do it. I never give a negative reference, but I won't be dishonest either. If I can't say positive things, I shouldn't be her reference. You don't want to choose someone you think loved your work only to discover too late that they didn't.

Some people choose a friend or trusted colleague on their current job. This is a bad idea. While you may have a good relationship with that person—or think you do—you never know when he or she might unintentionally mention your job search to someone else in your company. This could have negative repercussions for you, especially if you decide not to leave. It's a risk not worth taking.

Instead, you should maintain contact with previous coworkers. Maybe you only catch up with them via email or a short phone call once a year, but since you're on good terms and they know your work, they're the perfect people to use as references. Ask their permission first, of course, and then keep them on your go-to list. Just be sure to let them know when you're in an active job search and they may be getting a call. You should also remind them of experiences you've shared that they might refer to, such as projects you worked on together or teams you led.

If you're new to the job market, consider who might be able to attest to your work ethic. It could be a professor with whom you have a good relationship or someone who has observed your work as a volunteer.

When You Don't Get It

If you don't get this position, accept that it wasn't the right job at the right time, and remember there are plenty more options out there. Even though it can be disappointing to go through a long interview process and not come out with the win, it does happen. The best thing you can do is to learn from the experience. Call the recruiter or the human resources representative and ask for specific feedback on why you weren't the chosen candidate. Be open to receiving constructive criticism, and don't take it personally. Even if the information seems irrelevant or unfair, take what you can from it and use it to be better next time.

When you're unable to reach the recruiter or he simply doesn't give you anything helpful, you need to do your own self-assessment to figure out what you should've done differently. Sometimes you can do everything right and still not get the job, but you can almost always identify a question you could've answered more articulately, something you should tweak in your appearance, or a way to improve the way you connect with the interviewer. Review the information in this chapter, and be honest with yourself about areas in which you weren't quite at the standard you need to reach. Put in the work to be your best, stay positive, and keep looking. If you don't cave in and quit, you will land your dream job and earn the income you desire.

When They Want You

If they make you an offer, congratulations! Now you've just got a few more steps to go through before you can officially claim the position.

First and foremost, remember the job isn't yours until it's yours. Don't resign your current position or jump the gun by making announcements on social media until you've made it through the background checks and the offer is official. I have a friend who lost a job offer after a poppy seed muffin caused her to fail a drug test. You may not eat muffins, but there are other reasons the offer could fall through.

On that note, you can't put yourself in any situation where your job offer may be compromised. In other words, if someone else in your presence is smoking illegal substances, you need to remove yourself from the situation.

Drug tests aren't the only thing that can go wrong at this point. A gentleman I know lost an offer for his dream job when the company discovered he had a felony conviction. More than two decades had passed since he committed the offense, and he'd never had another run-in with the law. Because it stopped showing up on background checks after all that time, he almost forgot about it. However, this company's research was so thorough that they discovered the conviction and, as a consequence, withdrew the job offer. Unfortunately, this man had already resigned the position he'd held before the offer was made. The loss left him devastated, and what had promised to be a significant advancement for his career turned into the beginning of a long period of unemployment.

You may be breathing a sigh of relief because you don't have a criminal record and you can pass a drug test and financial background check with flying colors. I advise you not to get too comfortable. Things happen, so don't tender your resignation until you've completely locked down the new job. By completely locked down I mean making sure you have passed all background checks before giving your current employer a letter of resignation.

When You Resign

Regardless how you feel about your current company, there's no need to burn any bridges when you leave. While you may never want to return to that employer, you never know "who knows whom" in your industry or when someone from your old company might show up in just the place you want to be. Leave the same way you worked—with professionalism.

Be prepared for the fact that your employer may try to convince you to stay. Depending on the situation, you might even consider taking the offer. In my experience, though, when I've found a new position, a counteroffer usually won't make me stay. However, I did make an exception on one occasion.

I was leaving the company because my contributions weren't appreciated or rewarded, plain and simple. Sure, I got all the accolades and shiny plaques to hang on my wall, but you can't eat accolades and plaques don't pay the bills. No matter what I achieved I was overlooked for promotions. Never one to sit quietly and sulk, I went to my boss and asked if the new responsibilities I was taking on would make me eligible for a promotion. He said he couldn't make any promises, and it's a good thing he didn't. A year later I was doing more work, but I was still in the same position with no significant increase in my pay.

I'd had enough. I did what I do well and went out and found a job that would compensate me at the level my contributions deserved. When I gave my notice, my employers realized what they were losing, so much so that the CIO sat down with me to make a counteroffer. He apologized for the fact that the company had taken me for granted and assured me that it would never happen again. While it meant a lot to me that someone in his position would take time from his schedule to do that, it didn't change the fact that I'd been disrespected up to that point.

> *Give your resignation after you've been cleared for all pre-tests*

When I'm ready to leave, I'm ready to leave. It took my husband's calm, practical perspective to help me to see that the counteroffer really was better for me and my career as a whole. It's the only time I've accepted a counter. Decide before you give your notice whether or not you're open to staying and what it would take for you to do so. And don't be mad if no counter appears. It's not guaranteed, and you're moving on to something better anyway.

Making the Most of the Offer

You've done your research and you know what you should be paid for this new position. Even with this information in mind you haven't allowed anyone to nail you down on a specific number yet. Instead, you've stuck with a salary range knowing that everything is negotiable and benefits can be thrown in to sweeten the pot.

Remember to consider benefits such as vacation time, volunteer days, free training, or tuition reimbursement you currently receive when you're deciding what salary is acceptable. But you also need to consider what benefits you'll expect in this new opportunity. Depending on your position and the company, you may be able to negotiate any of the following:

- Additional vacation time
- Part-time or full-time telecommuting
- Gym or club memberships
- Stock options
- Signing bonus
- Company car
- Wardrobe allowance
- Relocation expenses
- Help selling your home
- Office redecorating allowance
- Upgraded business travel
- Potential bonuses
- Private school or college tuition for your children
- Other benefits specific to the industry

Often the key to successfully negotiating some of these perks is to tie them directly to your job. If you live in the same zip code as your new work site, don't expect them to pay for you to move a little closer. And if you're a front line employee, you can't go in demanding access to the company jet. Be reasonable and shrewd when you discuss benefits. Do your research and come prepared to ask for what you want.

Negotiating Salary

Of course, all the benefits in the world need to come attached to the right salary. At this point you should be focused on maximizing your starting salary, especially since that's the base from which bonuses will be paid and raises will be given.

If the initial offer isn't exactly what you want, don't panic. You can respond with something such as, "I'd really like to take advantage of this opportunity and be part of your team, but the salary is a little lower than I expected." That puts the ball in their court to start moving the number in the right direction.

Remember the unique value you bring to the table. By now you should know your professional worth and expect to be compensated accordingly. If you've done your due diligence in the job search and demonstrated what you can add to the company, you shouldn't feel you have to settle for less than you deserve. This is not the only job in the world. Remember, it's your responsibility to manage your career.

If there's no immediate progress but you're really interested in the position, ask for a day to think it over. You may be able to get the recruiter to lobby on your behalf, so feel her out and get her thoughts on the matter. It's in her interest for you to accept the position. Either way, know that the hiring manager may have to get permission to raise the offer by 10-15%, but that's usually what I ask for. If I've done my homework, we shouldn't be much farther apart.

Failing that, it may be time to negotiate some of the benefits listed above. Perhaps they only bring up the salary by 5%, but offer an outstanding signing bonus or increased vacation days. That may be worth taking, but you need to do the numbers and make sure you're not being short-changed.

This renegotiation is typically a one-shot deal. No asking for additional time. Come in knowing what you want and what you're willing to take. Sometimes you just have to get more creative to craft a win for both parties. Consider a client I worked with who received an offer that wouldn't even support his lifestyle. He wanted the position, but he couldn't afford to take it at that salary. If he'd turned it down, he would've regretted the lost opportunity.

I worked with him to come up with a solid counter—he'd take the position at the offered pay, but after ninety days his performance would be evaluated, and if it was merited, he'd receive an increase. They went for it. My client immediately went to work proving his worth. He did his job well, but he also shared recommendations for improvements that could benefit the company and checked in with his boss regularly to make sure his performance was on track. He worked his butt off for three months. I'm sure you can guess that when he reached the ninety-day mark he was rewarded with a well-deserved raise.

In my experience, men will ask for their money every time, but many women are afraid of hearing a no, so they'll either decline the offer without negotiating or worse, settle for what they can get. I used to be that way too. I trusted that I was being offered the best they could give and I took it, thinking I should just be happy to have the job. No more. Once I truly understood my worth I recalibrated my thinking to expect to be paid fairly for the value I'd bring to the table. If you're not quite there yet, keep working at it. In the meantime, fake it until you make it. When the time comes at least act like you know your value.

When the Offer Is Right on the Money

If the initial offer makes sense, let them know you appreciate it and you're excited about the chance to work for the company, still you'd like twenty-four hours to give it your full consideration before making a final decision. While they may be anxious to get you to commit, most people will respectfully allow you that time.

If they really put pressure on you to accept immediately, consider that a red flag. They've invested all this time and money in putting you through the interview process, so one day shouldn't be a big deal. If it is, you need to figure out why before you make your decision.

You don't need to wait a full twenty-four hours to call and accept the job. If you're secure in your decision, call back first thing in the morning. Thank them for the offer and explain that you'd like to accept it. Summarize your understanding of the terms so everyone is on the same page. Be very clear about what background checks need to be done before the position is officially yours and explain that you can't resign your current position until that's all taken care of. Typically, you'll receive a letter detailing the offer and explaining the process, but it's better to get the information up front.

Different companies have different policies. They may do drug testing, run a criminal records search, verify previous employment, or check your credit report. I once recruited a candidate with an Ivy League degree and experience with a Fortune 100 company. He was clearly the best candidate for the job and we made him an offer.

Excited to begin this new phase of his career, the candidate gave notice to his employer and prepared to start with us on a Monday. However, on the Friday before he was to begin his new role, his credit report came back, and his score was too low. The offer was rescinded. I lobbied on his behalf to no avail. It devastated me that I'd recruited this man, only to have him leave his former job and end up with nothing. He rebounded, but it was a challenging time for him. Don't let this happen to you.

When the time comes to sign a contract, be a stickler for the details. What's on that paper will dictate what you receive regardless what was discussed. My client Barbara learned this firsthand. When she received her contract she shared it with me. I don't typically do contract reviews because I am not a lawyer, but I'm glad I had the chance to look at that one.

The starting salary noted on the last page of the contract was higher than the salary on the first page. I advised her to make it clear that she was accepting the position based on the higher figure and to have the contract adjusted to reflect that. They didn't argue about it, but if she had missed it she could've lost out on the additional money. Pay attention to what you're signing and have a second pair of eyes look it over if you need to.

While this phase of the hiring process can go quickly, don't underestimate its importance. Take your time and be clear about your requirements. Don't settle for less than you deserve.

"If you want something you've never had, you must be willing to do something you've never done." — Thomas Jefferson

Read something that made you think, 'I should try this?' WRITE it down here. Once you finish the book, come back to this Reflection page and begin to create your plan to incorporate it into your life.

_____

_____

_____

_____

_____

_____

_____

_____

_____

_____

_____

_____

Determine

Recalibrate | verb | *to check and adjust by comparison to a standard; to determine and make corrections in.*

Determine

If you've read through this book, you know how important it is to clearly identify and strategically self-promote the unique value you bring to any workplace blessed enough to have you. You've started recalibrating your mindset to look at a job search as your opportunity to choose the right job for you rather than going into interviews simply hoping you'll be chosen. You've learned how to craft an interview-winning resume, handle any kind of interview with grace and professionalism, get the best job offer, and make the most of a job once you've landed it.

All that is wonderful. It's important. However, a career is a journey that, for most of us, lasts decades. If you start working in high school and continue through the typical retirement age, your career could last half a century. That's fifty years that will likely see you going from one position to another, and one company to another, many times over.

So how do you maintain your motivation to keep going when obstacles arise? How do you stay in it for the long haul? You determine what you want your career to look like. You determine how you'll go about achieving your goals. You determine not to quit until you attain them and you live by principles that help you stay on track. Below are several guidelines that have helped me stay focused through the many ups and downs of my career.

Career Success Principles

1. Maintain your positive mindset shift.
2. Remember your why.
3. Be persistent—don't give up.
4. Push beyond your comfort zone.
5. Speak success into your career.
6. Analyze feedback and choose what to act on.
7. Stop apologizing.
8. Balance and recharge.
9. Build your support system.
10. Never stop learning.

Maintain Your Positive Mindset Shift

If you're following the advice outlined in earlier chapters of this book, you're probably feeling pretty excited about all the changes you can make to uncover new career opportunities, position yourself as the desired candidate, and increase your salary. You now understand that you don't have to look at your job search from a place of desperation. You don't need to take every job offer that comes up or just be grateful to have any miserable job that provides a paycheck.

Because you've identified the unique value you bring to the marketplace, you're prepared to treat an interview as a two-way conversation. Yes, you want to impress them with your qualifications and your personality. However, they'll also have to impress you with their corporate culture, possibilities to do what you want to do at work, and the right salary. You're in a good headspace. It's important to stay there.

Your mindset is grounded in how you see yourself and what you think of yourself. Don't let inevitable setbacks or roadblocks change the fact that you know who you are and what you bring to the table better than anyone else. When doubts creep in, remember you're in control of your career. You always have options.

If you start to feel a sense of desperation or hopelessness creeping up, don't panic. Go back to the assessment work you did in the first section of this book. Remind yourself of your value and choose to do something to increase that value even further. And if you're still struggling, act as if you believe in yourself until you finally do.

Remember Your Why

It's been more than twenty years since I had to put back that $32 pair of Buster Browns I wanted for my son's first Easter. Those shoes meant a lot to me in the moment, but they were, of course, a symbol of something much more important. They represented my hunger to provide for my son. That hunger became my motivation to take charge of my career, ensure that I was fairly compensated, and take calculated risks to go farther faster.

I can't tell you what your why is. No one knows that but you. Maybe you've always had a desire to travel abroad and need a way to finance that dream. Perhaps you want to save enough money to start your own business, pay for a house or a new car with cash, or just be able to live debt-free. There may be a nonprofit organization you want to support, or maybe you have aging parents whose lives you want to make more comfortable.

Your why is your own and no one can tell you that your motivation is right or wrong. If you've longed to own a collection of red-bottomed shoes and that longing is enough to keep you motivated, then hold on to that. Stick a photo of those dream shoes on your mirror or on a vision board, and go for it. As long as the aspiration, whatever it is, is strong enough to capture your imagination and keep you motivated, you don't need to justify it to anyone.

When you face challenges in your career, and you will, go back to your why. It should be compelling enough to propel you to ask for a raise when you deserve one, apply for stretch jobs when the opportunities arise, and be willing to speak up about your abilities and your accomplishments so you can be acknowledged and rewarded accordingly.

My why has driven much of my career decision-making. When I was in full-time ministry my husband and I enrolled our son in a public school. Until then he had been in private school, but I was only getting $100 a month from my church. The package I received when I left my previous corporate job was running out and my husband was left covering all our overhead. My money was so tight I had to rotate getting my hair and nails done. There was no way I could afford to do both at the same time. I was out telling people how great God is, but I wasn't living in that abundance.

My drastically reduced income also meant private school was no longer an option, so my husband took our son to his zoned public high school to register him. When they came back I could sense something was clearly wrong. "I just can't do it," James told me. "If you went up there, you'd understand." It was far from the kind of environment we wanted our son exposed to every day.

I immediately went to work trying to get our son enrolled in one of the better high schools in our county. I reached out to everyone all the way up to the school superintendent. When I finally connected with him he made it clear that no exception would be made. "Your child will never go to that school," he told me. Trying to reason with the many layers of that bureaucracy was a waste of time.

I didn't care what that man said. I knew there was always a way and I wasn't going to let anyone or anything stop me from providing for my son. I made the decision to go back to work full-time and I landed a job making more money per hour than I'd ever made up to that point in my career. I earned enough to allow us to rent an apartment in the better school zone and we maintained that apartment for four years, until our son graduated from high school. It certainly cost less than private school tuition, but if I hadn't gone back to corporate work it would've been out of reach.

Whatever your why, hold on to it and use it as your motivation when doors seem to be closing in your face and all your battles seem to be uphill. If it's really important to you, your why can give you the courage and determination to accomplish more than you've imagined possible.

Be Persistent — Don't Give Up

You leave your final interview feeling you've connected with everyone from the HR representative to the hiring manager and her peers who sat on the panel. You answered every question with a brilliant response, asked your own well-thought-out questions and charmed everyone with your professional, but warm and approachable personality. You even shared a laugh or two with your interviewers and discovered that you and the hiring manager belonged to the same sorority. The look she gave you on the way out the door seemed to say, "You've got this." It's just a matter of time, you figure, before you get the offer. But it doesn't come. It turns out they've decided to go with another candidate.

Unfortunately, you can do everything right and still not get the job. It happens to all of us for any number of reasons. Sometimes the leadership team already has an internal candidate in mind for the job. Sometimes there's a candidate with a personal connection she can exploit to put her over the top. Sometimes that job wasn't meant for you and something better is coming along. There will always be parts of the process you can't control.

I've seen so many people get depressed because the job search drags on longer than they think it should. Even worse, some people completely give up because they lose out on the one job they think is the perfect opportunity—as if that's the only job in the world. The problem is when you fall into a funk you can't be your best on the job or in an interview. You start to doubt your value, your energy drops, and you have trouble selling yourself. If you don't believe you can be an asset to the company, you can't expect your boss or interviewers to believe it.

So how do you stay focused and determined in the face of rejection and disappointment? For me, and for many of my clients, it comes down to a matter of faith. I trust God when He says He will never withhold anything good from me. When you don't get a job you thought you really should have, you have to acknowledge that it wasn't for you. Maybe you weren't ready for it. Maybe there's something better coming your way. Maybe you're being protected from an environment that would have been detrimental to you or to your career.

As I mentioned earlier, a friend of mine went through a long interview process with a Fortune 100 company and she landed the job. Unfortunately, the day of the required drug test, she enjoyed a poppy seed muffin. As many of us now know, poppy seeds can cause opiates to be detected in drug testing, and that's exactly what happened to her. She failed the drug test and the company rescinded the job offer.

Naturally, she was upset. It would've been easy for her to feel like a victim, fall into a depression, and just give up. After all, she hadn't done anything wrong, and the job had been snatched right out of her hands. But she persisted, and in the end, she actually landed a better position with a great company. This new job allowed her to leave a significant imprint on the organization and effect transformational change in a way she never would've been able to in the position she lost. When she tells her story, she always explains that she believes God allowed her to fail that drug test because He had something greater waiting for her.

Whatever your religion, if you're a person of faith, you know God's promises to you, and with those promises to rely on, you simply can't quit. If you don't subscribe to any particular religion, then nurture a belief that the universe is a place of abundance and you're just as deserving of your share as anyone else. Either way, prepare yourself for the fact that your job search and your career will have ups and downs, failures and successes, rejection and approval. Do what you can to tip the scales in favor of the positive, and whatever you do, never give up on your dreams and goals.

Push Beyond Your Comfort Zone

From the outside looking in, the average person might wonder how I've managed to build a fulfilling, challenging career and consistently increase my salary. One of the keys to my success is that I learned early to push beyond my comfort zone. Walking into my boss's office to ask for a raise for the first time wasn't a comfortable experience, but I did it, and it paid off. I've gone after jobs with full knowledge that I'd have to learn new skills in order to succeed. I've landed positions that listed a college degree as a minimum requirement even though I didn't have one, and was honest about that fact. (As I write this, I'm back in school finishing my degree, but I'm doing that for my personal satisfaction.) Let's face it. Many people in my situation wouldn't have even bothered to apply.

What one thing motivates you to push beyond your comfort zone? Is that your why?

I'm currently coaching a young woman who wants to make the leap to management.

When we first met, she didn't really believe that type of advancement was possible for her because she didn't have any management experience to speak of. But everyone has to start somewhere. As we reviewed her work background, we talked about all the different leadership experience she's had, including managing teams of people on specific projects. It turns out she has demonstrated management skills in a variety of ways, even though she's never held a title of manager. She doesn't feel totally ready, but I'm encouraging her to go ahead and apply for management-level positions anyway. I'm sure she'll land one and handle the new responsibilities well.

The better prepared you are the more confident you'll feel and the easier it will be for you to get yourself out of your comfort zone when you need to in order to take advantage of opportunities. Too many women are underpaid and underemployed because they feel they have to meet every single requirement for a job before they apply for it or wait for the yearly merit increase and hope they get more money. Everything laid out in the Adjust section of this book is there to give you the tools and the confidence to break out of your comfort zone. Do it.

Speak Success into Your Career

Not long ago, I went on vacation and told my team not to bother emailing me because I wouldn't be checking my inbox, however, if anyone had a real emergency they could always call me. When I got a text message from a team member who wanted to know if I could talk, I didn't rush to call her. She hadn't said it was an emergency, so I finished my morning workout and got dressed. When I finally reached her, she was in a panic. She'd made a mistake at work and she was terrified what the fallout might be. "I just don't feel like I can do this job," she said.

I assured her she could, in fact, do the job, since she'd already successfully handled similar responsibilities without the title or the compensation. Everyone makes mistakes. Her blunder wasn't a fatal one, but she was insecure, and she was speaking those insecurities into her career. She'd developed the habit of saying, "This job is overwhelming." One day she said it in front of my boss and he pulled me aside to question whether we'd made a bad hire. I covered for her as best I could by explaining that was just the way she talked, but it put me in a bad position since I was the one who brought her on and it made her look bad. She was diminishing herself in the eyes of her peers and in the eyes of upper-level management.

On the other hand, as a hiring manager I find that male job candidates are much more likely to brag about their accomplishments. It's almost as if many of the female candidates think what's on their resume is enough and to highlight something great about themselves might seem boastful. But watch a couple of middle-aged, out-of-shape men playing a game of one-on-one on the basketball court. Even though they're out of breath, their knees are aching, and their backs are tight, they're still talking trash about how they're the greatest players the game has ever seen. For many men, boasting comes easily. It's ingrained in them by our culture. Too many women, on the other hand, have a tendency to be self-deprecating. You expect your excellence to speak for itself. Or worse, you run yourself down or diminish your accomplishments as "no big deal." After all, you're only doing your job, right?

Wrong. It's your responsibility to let people know what's uniquely valuable about you. When you try to turn attention away from your achievements out of some sense of false humility you lose an opportunity to demonstrate why a company should hire you, pay you more, and treat you well to keep you content. You show people what to think of you. The way you dress and the way you behave create a certain image, but you can destroy the best image of yourself with your words. Focus on the positive in any situation and give voice to that. Speak about yourself as a competent professional with confidence and pride.

Analyze Feedback and Choose What to Act On

I'm always interested in any critical feedback that can help me improve my professional performance. You should be too. It's invaluable to hear what your strengths are so you can make the most of them. It's also important to know where you're weak so you can make necessary improvements. You don't have to wait for quarterly or annual reviews to get some insight. From your resume and interviewing skills to your current job performance and professional persona, you can get valuable input from trusted advisors, colleagues, a mentor, or a coach.

> *It's your responsibility to tell people what's uniquely valuable about you.*

The trick to using feedback wisely is developing the ability to judge when you should make real changes and when you should either ignore it or find a way around it. I've consistently gotten positive feedback about my professional attire, for example. It reinforces my belief that this is an area I've mastered and it makes a difference, so I continue to create the most polished image for myself that I can.

I've also gotten critical feedback that has inspired me to make improvements. Early in this book I mentioned I worked as a journalist at one time and my colleague's feedback made me a much stronger writer. An HR rep once pointed out to me that my answers to interview questions were long-winded, so I turned my attention to crafting more succinct responses. Being concise may never be my greatest strength, but I've made the effort to improve in that area. No matter how far I advance in my career I'll always remain open to insights that can make me better at what I do.

Feedback from other parties is an important tool in your professional development, but you must use your own judgment to decide how to react to it. Don't automatically believe every criticism you get and jump to correct it. First, take emotion out of the equation and analyze the information as objectively as you possibly can. Is it similar to feedback you've gotten in the past? Is it something you already had an inkling you should improve? If you're really honest with yourself, can you see some truth in the criticism? When the HR rep told me I went on too long with my answers to questions, I could see the validity of the comment. I do like to talk and I can get carried away when I'm passionate about the subject. The feedback was honest and helpful.

Next, consider the source of the criticism. If the comment comes from someone with whom you have a contentious relationship, you have to question whether or not it's legitimate and look at his or her motives. However, you should always remember that someone who doesn't seem to like you personally may still have enough objectivity to share helpful observations. In other words, they don't have to like you in order to notice what you can do better.

Lastly, put any feedback you get into perspective. While it may come from a good place, it's still up to you to analyze whether it's your truth and what you should do about it. Let me give you an example. A mentee of mine told me she really wanted to become a project manager. She had applied to a project management training program with her employer, but she'd been denied because, according to the feedback, she was too quiet and her voice was too soft. The decision-makers told her a project manager needed to have the loudest voice in the room in order to command respect, and that would never be her. "I do speak softly," she admitted.

I asked her, "Do you agree that you have to be the loudest voice in the room?" She said she did because this man (who had a very masculine view of leadership) had told her so.

While that may be one style of managing effectively, it's certainly not the only way. I shared with her how I'd had a professor at Georgia State University during my junior year who's told me I'd never be a journalist. I could've listened to that analysis and decided to do something else, but instead, I persisted. When I wrote my first article for The Atlanta Journal-Constitution, I went back to the school and slid a copy of the article under the professor's office door. She couldn't have been more wrong about me and I wanted her to know it.

It's never my responsibility to tell a coaching client, mentee, or team member they can't have the job of their dreams. My obligation is to tell them what they need to do to get there. In keeping with that belief, I asked this woman if she believed she had what it takes to become a project manager. She said she did, but thought she'd have to become louder and more outspoken in order to get there. I pointed out that she was already warm and engaging, powerful tools for leadership. Instead of trying to change something so fundamental to her nature, I encouraged her to make the most of the fact that some teams need to be led by a quieter voice.

My mentee had to take the feedback and use it in the way that best suited her. Rather than trying to speak more loudly, she simply had to demonstrate that her quiet self could still lead with confidence. Not every team needs a loud-talking leader, but every organization can benefit from a diverse workforce. I'm excited to share that this young woman was able to demonstrate her leadership abilities and was offered an entry-level project manager role at her current company. Her employer is investing in her by paying for project manager training courses.

Stop Apologizing

This may seem a strange principle to live by, but it's important. If you wrong someone you should, of course, apologize. But many women have made apologizing a way of life. You say you're sorry for every little thing even when it isn't really your fault. Stop it. Just stop, especially in the workplace. It makes you look weak and unsure of yourself—and you are neither. Your intentions may be good. Maybe you're trying to own up to what you've done. Maybe you're trying to protect a coworker from blame or avoid hurting someone's feelings. There are better ways to do all that.

Here's the deal. You should own your mistakes and be accountable for your decisions and your actions. But you need to be careful about the way you take ownership of what you've done. If you observe men in a professional environment, you'll notice they rarely apologize for anything. Instead, they tend to correct a mistake and assure everyone it'll never happen again. They don't feel a need to publicly flog themselves because they've messed up. They commit to fixing it and move on.

I'm not saying you need to try to be "one of the guys" when you're at the office, but there are several things we can learn from men about how to be successful in corporate America, and this is one of them. I too used to apologize excessively, so I'm speaking from experience. Save it for when it really matters. You'll command more respect when you minimize your use of "I'm sorry" in the office.

Balance and Recharge

Your career is an important part of your life. If anyone believes that, I certainly do, and the reality is that most of us spend more time at work than we do at home with our families. Yes, your job is, and should be, an important component of your life. But wait. There's more.

I work long hours and when I'm in the office I'm on. However, I'm quite clear on the fact that I also have to take care of myself. I have to practice the kinds of healthy self-care habits that help me find peace and reinvigorate me so I can be my best self for my family, for my employer, and for me. There are times I get out of balance, but I have specific strategies to rebalance myself.

Here are a few restorative practices that can help you manage the stress of a demanding career.

- Meditation
- Prayer
- Deep breathing exercises
- Long soaks in the bath
- Journaling
- Gratitude journaling
- Regular exercise
- Healthy food choices
- Vacation time
- Sufficient sleep
- Visualization exercises
- Gardening
- Arts or crafts
- Upbeat or uplifting music
- Time spent in nature
- Play or recreation of any kind

Anything that takes your mind off work, especially done with a meditative state of mind, is wonderful for reducing stress and allowing you to rebalance. As I write this, adult coloring books are all the rage, and the publishers' marketing angle is that coloring is a great way to relax. Some people bake or clean when they need to unwind. Others watch comedies and laugh away the stress.

Figure out what you can do that will leave you feeling renewed and make it a regular practice. Recognize that when you feel so overwhelmed you think there's no way you can find five minutes for any of your relaxation techniques, that's the time you most need them.

Build Your Support System

When I made the decision to go full force in my career I knew there was no way I could arrive at the office every morning at nine and pull out of the parking lot at five. With the industries I worked in—and frankly, most industries—it would be incredibly difficult to get ahead that way. I knew I'd have to make a habit of coming in early and staying late.

However, I had a young son at home and he required attention. Someone needed to be there to help him with homework, go on his class field trips, and get him back and forth to soccer practice. I could occasionally do some of those things, but there was no way I could commit to being the kind of parent who took on that responsibility alone every day.

Instead, my husband and I decided we would work as a team. James left his job every day at 5:00 to take our son to soccer. He took primary responsibility for the day-to-day drop-offs and pick-ups, and he put many of his career aspirations on hold to do it. Now that our son is an adult,

Take care of your whole self: Mind, Body and Spirit.

James has the chance to pursue more of his goals, and he's doing that. But had he not been willing to delay those dreams, I would never have been able to pursue mine. My husband has been my primary support throughout my career and we can now support each other as we each follow our professional ambitions.

You should do what you can to get your family behind you, but even when that's not an option you can still build your support team in lots of ways. Join a networking group or industry organization and build relationships of mutual support. Join or start a mastermind group. Find a mentor or hire a coach. Take a workshop and network with other attendees. Look for accountability or support groups on social media networks. With the Internet, your options to connect are endless, but don't neglect real-world opportunities either.

Never Stop Learning

The fact that you've read this book demonstrates that you're open to expanding your way of thinking and willing to implement new ideas to develop your career. That's good because the minute you think you know everything about anything you start to stagnate in that area. I teach people how to navigate their careers for a living, but I'm always studying, reading, and observing for my own sake and for the sake of my clients.

This book provides you a wealth of information about how you can conduct an effective job search or make the most of the job you have. However, that's not enough. You must continue to develop your skills and your industry knowledge. Continue to observe and emulate people who've already attained what you're working to get. Take classes and workshops. Read books and articles that give you specific career knowledge or expand your thinking. The learning should never stop.

If you'd like to discover more about how you can recalibrate your professional life to land your dream job and earn a higher salary, visit me at YvetteGavin.com. I have free resources there that will help you with this process. Your career is a journey with twists and turns, starts and stops, and the occasional obstacle you have to overcome. However, when you're willing to do the work and recalibrate when necessary you can achieve the kind of professional success you've only begun to dream of.

"If you want something you've never had, you must be willing to do something you've never done." — Thomas Jefferson

Read something that made you think, 'I should try this?' WRITE it down here. Once you finish the book, come back to this Reflection page and begin to create your plan to incorporate it into your life.

_____

_____

_____

_____

_____

_____

_____

_____

_____

_____

_____

_____

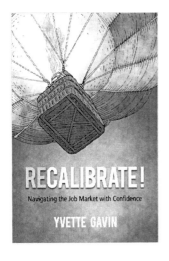

We invite you to continue your experience with Recalibrate! Navigating the Job Market with Confidence at our website: **YvetteGavin.com**

- Share how you feel about Recalibrate! and read what others are saying
- Share your insights and discuss the book with other readers on the Recalibrate Forum
- Communicate with the Author
- Read Yvette's Blog
- Get FREE template downloads

Connect with Yvette:

linkedin.com/in/yvette-gavin

facebook.com/yvettegavinrelationships

twitter.com/yvettegavin

For information about having the author speak to your organization or group, please contact us at yvettegavin.com or by phone at 424-262-2462

Yvette Recommended Resource

Job loss is one of the most significant stresses a person can face. Upon learning about a layoff, almost every area of life is affected. While each person is impacted in unique ways, certain areas of life are inevitably changed to some degree or another.

There is a vast amount of information out there to help people who are unemployed. The problem is how to find it. This book targets those who have lost a job or been selected for layoff. The various tips contained herein also relate to individuals who just want to save money by cutting personal/home expenses.

As you process the news of a job layoff, Getting Beyond the Day™ is a roadmap to help you stay focused on finding your next career move, but also addressing all of the other aspects of your life. It contains valuable resources to pursue as aids during your time of unemployment. Use the Getting Beyond the Day™ Workbook as your daily notebook to keep track of your accomplishments and "to do" items. The book is broken down into three main sections: Career, Family, and Life, with resources relating to each and words of wisdom from a hiring manager, an executive, and a person who has experienced unemployment. In addition, appendices outline other tips.

Ordering Information

ISBN 978-0-9860159-2-2

Retail Price: $14.99

Contact Information

Nicole Antoinette

nicole@gettingbeyondtheday.com

678.232.6156

gettingbeyondtheday.com

About the Author

Yvette Gavin is driven by a deep conviction and passion to help others grow spiritually and professionally. Her career and life's work covers a board spectrum of successes that speaks highly of her talent and commitment to excellence. Yvette is a leader, ordained minister, author, and coach who has hosted television programs, conducted international training workshops and local conferences, and has appeared on radio and TV programs as a Communications expert.

From managing teams to directing an organization, Yvette is known for her ability to build high-performing Information Technology (IT) teams that deliver exceptional quality. Yvette has held progressive leadership roles at Lockheed-Martin Aeronautical, Delta Air Lines, AT&T, Cbeyond and Cox Communications. Prior to her IT career, Yvette was a reporter for the Atlanta Journal Constitution and the Birmingham (ALA) News. At CNN Headline News (HLN), Yvette progressed from an editor's position to manager of the Southeastern Bureau where she was responsible for the day-to-day production of local news stories. It's safe to say that Yvette knows a thing or two about how to navigate a career across a changing landscape and land a highly rewarding job that yields a desirable income.

In 1997, Yvette founded Sisterhood, a Christian women's mentoring organization. In 2002, she wrote the inspiring book, What to do After you Say I Do, while serving as an assistant pastor at Crosswords Christian Community Church in Lithonia, Ga. Yvette was drawn to the teaching profession as a child, and for years, while maintaining a full-time corporate leadership position, she has provided one-on-one and group coaching in the areas of career development and spiritual growth. Yvette is also a powerful keynote speaker who has spoken on various community platforms.

Combining her passion and experience of building thriving workplace and personal relationships, Yvette formed, Yvette Gavin Consulting, a Communications Consulting firm that provides business consulting and personal coaching services through dynamic training programs. Some of Yvette's most noted work has been for the United States Government. In 2012, Yvette conducted a workplace relationship workshop for the U.S. Consulate in Brazil, and has facilitated numerous marriage workshops for the Georgia National Guard. She has an incredible heart for helping others achieve their dreams.

Yvette studied Journalism at Georgia State University and holds B.S. degrees (2016) from Oral Roberts University in Tulsa, OK. Yvette is the recipient of various leadership and community awards. In 2007, the Georgia National Guard Chaplaincy Corp bestowed upon Yvette the Exemplary Performance Award while serving as an instructor for the Strong Bonds Marriage Conference. She later received the Leadership Excellence Coin in 2010 from the 78th Aviation Troop Command for her dedication to providing relationship training to Georgia's Soldiers. Yvette is also the recipient of the State of Georgia Governor's Award for Outstanding Leadership.

In 2015, Yvette was appointed Program Lead for Cox's inaugural Women's Employee Resource Group (ERG), and the recipient of the Cox Communications' Process Improvement Award in 2014. Yvette is a member of the International Christian Coaching Association and is a certified PREP trainer, and life coach.

Spend any considerable amount of time with Yvette, and you will quickly discern the two most important things in her life--- her relationship with God and her relationship with her family. Yvette has been married to James for 29 years. They have an adult son, Jamison.

Yvette Gavin Consulting

Yvette Gavin Consulting is based in Atlanta, Georgia. The foundational purpose of the firm is to teach and encourage personal growth through a variety of customized and highly engaging presentations, including keynotes, seminars, workshop, and coaching. Called the inspirational leader, Yvette specializes in transformational change that helps individuals and businesses to move from where they are to where they want to be. Yvette has an incredible heart for helping others achieve their dreams. Where her approach has proven to be successful for men and women, Yvette's particular focus is on helping women grow their careers, businesses, and spiritual lives.

Keynotes, Seminars, and Webinars
- Navigating the Job Market with Confidence
- Resume Writing 101
- The Interview

Coaching
- Leadership Coaching
- Career Coaching
- Spiritual Growth Coaching

Training and Consulting
Organizational consulting focused on communication, management, and transformation using the following approaches:

- Purchase Approach
- Doctor-Patient Approach
- Process Approach

Other Material by Yvette

Have you ever wondered why some people seem to have happy marriages while others do not? Is the difference found in their education, intelligence, financial status, social status, physical appearance, or sex appeal? The truth is: None of the above! What To Do After You Say I Do is two books in one. It reveals the missing link between wanting a successful marriage and achieving it! In Part I, Yvette Gavin shares the secrets that have kept her marriage strong, thriving, and fulfilling for more than 28 years. These are the tools and techniques she teaches in one-on-one coaching sessions that have yielded great success for others. In Part II, which includes expanded material added since the first edition, Yvette offers a unique opportunity to immediately begin applying the principles that lead to a healthy, thriving, fulfilling marriage — along with a daily devotional.

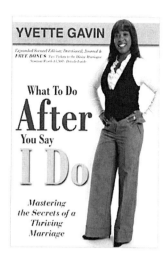

To purchase:

Amazon.com/Yvette-Gavin

Follow Yvette on Amazon to get new release updates, read my blog posting, and more!

CPSIA information can be obtained
at www.ICGtesting.com
Printed in the USA
FFOW01n1526250217
32631FF